THE DEVIL WAS LISTENING

Stanley G. Rothenberg

The Devil Was Listening
by Stanley G. Rothenberg

Copyright 2018 Stanley G. Rothenberg
Published by: Stanley G. Rothenberg
justiceforstanrothenberg.com

Stanley G. Rothenberg
12726 Glenkirk Road
Henrico, VA 23233-2251

ISBN: 978-0-9997465-0-9 (print)
ISBN: 978-0-9997465-1-6 (ebook)

First printing:

THE DEVIL WAS LISTENING

Stanley G. Rothenberg

How Stanley G. Rothenberg, a sixty-four-year-old man, was
sentenced to life in prison for talking dirty on the internet

Contents

Introduction

JUSTICE CAN BE a fickle bitch.

Four hundred years ago, witches were burned at the stake for sorcery. Fifty years ago, it was illegal to serve alcohol to "known homosexuals." Five years ago, marijuana was illegal in all fifty states.

Not so long ago, depression and insanity were prima facie evidence of demonic possession or unthinkable evil, not chemical imbalances. Shell shock was the result of cowardice instead of traumatic brain injury and post-traumatic stress disorder.

Why? Why do the standards by which we evaluate criminal behavior change?

Blame science.

New evidence yields insights into human nature and forces us to recognize that what we once classified as wrong or evil or aberrant may be just on the far end of the spectrum of normal behavior. Maybe someday judges and juries will be able to peer directly into the hearts and souls of the accused and determine the true intent of every defendant, but until that day, our courts stand on shifting sands of public policy and ever-changing inchoate sense of right and wrong.

Nowhere is that more true than in the case of *United States v. Stanley G. Rothenberg*.

The facts of Stan's case are straightforward. Stan, a life-long out-of-the-closet gay man struggling with erectile dysfunction, found people talking "pervy" arousing. In order to satisfy that desire, he visited online chat rooms, seeking out more extreme "pervy" talk. One day, he struck up a conversation with a man who claimed to be having sex with his eleven-year-old mentally handicapped daughter. Stan found the conversation titillating—not the details of the act, but the fact that the father was disclosing his conduct—and wanted more. When the father agreed to meet up to discuss "sharing" his daughter with Stan, Stan agreed, excited by the opportunity to talk dirty face-to-face with the father. He wanted nothing to do with the daughter.

There was no handicapped eleven-year-old daughter. There was no daughter at all. The father was an undercover detective skilled and practiced at seducing child molesters on the internet.

Moreover, Stan had never had sex with a female. He had no interest in children. His interest in the non-existent daughter was no more real than she was.

Then how did Stanley G. Rothenberg end up with a life sentence for talking dirty on the internet?

In 2008, a confluence of prejudices collided to yield profound injustice. First, in a failed attempt to make sentences uniform across the nation, the federal Sentencing Guidelines were mandatory, effectively crippling the traditional power of judges to fashion punishments to fit crimes. Second, courts were just coming to understand the profound impact that long-term abuse of prescribed benzodiazepines had on the human psyche. Finally, the rise of the internet brought with it a host of demonized behaviors and preferences. Child pornography exploded on the scene. The mere act of talking about a forbidden act was conflated to be intent to commit a criminal act.

Today, there are thousands of men like Stanley Rothenberg—"sex offenders" who never touched a child—rotting away in federal prison, banished from society by politically driven and increasingly controversial mandatory Sentencing Guidelines. The sheer magnitude of the injustice is immediately evident in the sentencing matrix attached to the end of this book.

High-profile offenders who actually abuse children—people like Jared Fogle—get sentenced to a few years in prison, if that, even when their cases involved serious and long-term damage to children. But people like Stan, who have never even touched a child, are sacrificed on the altar of political correctness and sentenced to life in prison.

This is Stan's story.

PART I

CRIME

One

===

HOW HAD IT come to this?

Stanley Rothenberg—Stan to his friends—stared out over the Atlantic Ocean, coffee cup in hand, watching the sun splatter across the calm sea. From his high-rise condo balcony, the sea stretched out, limitless, its peaceful surface barely marred by waves and the faint skittering of yachts across it.

Not only the rich sought out the sea. Charter boats plowed through the water, carrying tourists on expeditions, steering around commercial fishing boats taking advantage of the long season. May was one of the best fishing months of the year, and everything from Amberjack to Blackfin tuna was running. Closer in, surfers coaxed rides out of the relatively flat sea, showing off for the tourists crowding the beaches now vacated by the spring break hoards.

Ashore, Fort Lauderdale was waking up. The sprawling metropolis perched on the southeast coast of Florida was just thirty miles north of Miami the boundary was marked by little more than road signs now. The sky was a brilliant blue, the result of a brisk wind from the north, shifting from the northwest overnight, blowing pollution off the coast and to the south. A faint haze had cleared off early. Later in the day, as the winds shifted to the northeast, the sky would be overcast as it brought in the moisture from the sea, but for the moment, it was a stunning, clear blue.

Fort Lauderdale in 2008 was everything Stan had ever wanted: the perfect life with the perfect home and a graceful retirement with the perfect love of his life.

He and David had worked so long and so hard for this. It had been tough, even with his family's support, to build their furniture store business, to make it the toast of the town, and to build a stable and successful business. David had been the insanely-creative half of their home furnishing business, Stan the backroom frugal soul who made sure it all worked. Together, they had been unstoppable.

It had been their dream, *theirs*, to retire to the Florida coast and spend their lives together in a warm, diverse society. They would grow old together, gracefully transcending the disdain the gay community showed its older members.

So what if they were no longer the young, stunning studs they'd been when they'd first met? They'd still have each other.

Outwardly, everything was perfect. Stan's stunning condo, bought at an as-is price, had been exquisitely renovated and decorated. He had friends, causes that he fought for, a daily routine he found satisfying, and enough money to live very comfortably.

Back in Virginia, he'd been a respected member of the community and involved in local government, and he had already stepped up to take on some responsibilities in his new neighborhood. His current partner was devilishly handsome and well-built. There was even a Dunkin' Donuts nearby so he could get the perfect cup of coffee anytime he wanted it.

Perfect.

Except for one missing piece: David.

The cold, hard ache ran through him again. Everyone said it would get better with time, but it hadn't. No matter how he tried to move on, to accept the fact of David's death, a large part of his life had gone to the grave with David.

Staying in Richmond hadn't been an option. Every street, every building, every season reminded him of what he'd lost. Without David, his anchor, he was adrift, battered by life and fighting off the free-floating anxiety as best he could alone.

One day, the answer came to him: Florida.

He'd go back to the brilliant sun and palm trees, the overheated erotic nightlife, and the hordes of gorgeous, hard-bodied young men who lived there. Back to Florida, where he'd lost his virginity, and where he'd been introduced to the benzodiazepines that held his chronic crippling anxiety at bay, where he'd met David Jacks, the man who had been his life partner for twenty-four years.

Florida, where his life had finally made sense. Perhaps it would make sense again.

Stan had felt a profound sense of relief when he finally made the decision to move back to Florida. Telling his family had been easy—they all understood the aching void David's death had left in his soul. It was his brother-in-law, Joel, who'd nailed it when he'd asked, "About this move back to Florida—were you looking for David again?"

Stan had paused for a moment before giving the only answer that made any sense to him. "How could I not?"

■　■　■

Stan Rothenberg was born in Richmond, Virginia, on April 11, 1944, the second son in a large, working class but striving Jewish family that had put down roots in Virginia a generation earlier. His father, Joseph "Joe" Rothenberg, operated a low-end furniture business with his two brothers. The store—D. S. Rothenberg and Sons—had been founded by Stanley's grandfather, David Samuel Rothenberg, at the turn of the century. The store was in Shockoe Bottom, a working class enclave dotted with storefronts and small businesses, many still operated by families who lived nearby or above their dry cleaners, bakeries, groceries, and apparel shops.

In the post-war era, the American South was not unwelcoming to its Jewish citizens. Charleston, South Carolina's Jewish community dates back to the seventeenth century. Southern Jews took up for the Confederacy. Judah P. Benjamin, the first Jewish US senator, served as Jefferson Davis's Secretary of State. In the mid–twentieth century, Jim Crow-style discrimination and Ku Klux Klan-inspired terror were not things that Jews in the South worried about. Anti-Semitism was real but muted.

While Jews might have been tolerated in the South, homosexuals were not. There were laws on the books prohibiting selling alcohol to "known homosexuals." In the very proper and rigid Virginia culture, a gay family member was a shameful secret, a sin visited on the family for some wrongdoing in the past.

From Stan's earliest days, he suffered from crippling

anxiety. He could never decide whether it was a result of social pressures or his upbringing. It affected his life in a number of ways. An avid baseball fan, with the long, lanky build of a good player, the terror of having to play in front of a crowd warred with his profound enjoyment of the sport. Rather than trying out for the team, Stan volunteered to be the manager for teams in both high school and in college.

Anxiety also kept him a virgin. He stayed so through high school and college and the first years of his career as an epidemiologist for the US Public Health Service, until he requested a transfer to Miami. There, with the steamy society and treatment from a good psychiatrist including a prescription for Valium—he blossomed. It was in Miami that he finally felt normal. It was in Miami that he lost his virginity and met David Jacks. And it was to Miami that he would return to resurrect himself.

■ ■ ■

Jaded by the age he grew up in, numbed by his lifelong dependence on benzodiazepines, and frustrated by erectile dysfunction, Stan finally stumbled across the last frontier of sexual playgrounds: the internet chat room.

Like so many others in the late 90s, Stan found that America Online made things easy. No, he didn't understand much about ISPs and websites and bytes, but he didn't have to in order to use AOL. The menus and search boxes were easy to use, the technicians who walked him through his early internet fam flights were courteous, and soon Stan found himself surfing the web with everyone else.

Well, perhaps not so much surfing—more like wading

in the increasingly-deep pool of AOL-provided resources. Very early in his exploration, he found the AOL chat rooms.

There were two things that were absolutely true about Stan Rothenberg. First, he was unequivocally a gay man. He had never had an interest in females and indeed found the concept of sex with a female repulsive. Nor was he interested in children, bestiality, or any of a number of odd perversions that lurk in the darker corners of the internet.

Second, to call him jaded would be an understatement. His crippling life-long anxiety and subsequent dependence on benzodiazepines blunted his arousal instincts. Couple that with normal senior erectile dysfunction, and Stan faced difficulty getting turned on by anything at all.

But in the chat room, Stan found something that turned him on, a practice that cut through the dullness of his life like the sharpest virtual knife in the universe. Unable to perform physically, and trapped by his circumstances, Stan reached out to the fringes of the sexual continuum to people who *were* truly perverted and found that *their excitement over their activities*—not the activity itself—sliced through the blunted affect of his life and touched something he thought he'd lost forever. He called it "pervy talk."

At some level, Stan believed that the anonymity of using a screen names and being able to log into a chat room provided a measure of privacy. After all, the chat rooms were hosted on AOL, and anybody with an account could sign in. Sure, he understood that actually performing the acts they chatted about were illegal, at least some them. But he didn't see anything illegal about "pervy talk" with strangers. It was allowed, wasn't it? AOL had chat rooms set up for it, and it wasn't like he was actually going to do anything.

Stan reached out to these faceless people typing end-less abbreviated scrawls in anonymous AOL chat lines and said—in essence—talk dirty to me.

He had no idea who was listening.

Two

2008
Fort Lauderdale, Florida

═══════════════════════════════

THE SHORT, BALDING, pudgy detective leaned back in his chair and smiled. The vindication in his grin belied the cherubic cast to his features. It was not a pretty sight. "Got you now, don't I?" he said, tapping on the sheaf of papers in front of him.

It was finally here, the response to the subpoena demanding records from America Online. Now there was a real person attached to the screen name *LuvYngB-Butts*, not just some shadowy figure creeping out of the filthy online chat rooms. The individual who'd taken his bait had a name: Stanley G. Rothenberg.

Many defendants had made the mistake of underestimating Detective Neil Spector. It was easy to overlook the intensity in his dark eyes and ignore his determined focus on his prey. It was personal to him, this business of putting tracking down and convicting perverts who targeted children.

Spector started stalking internet sex offenders in 2005, when he'd been assigned to the Internet Crimes Against Children task force (ICAC), a joint federal, state, and local law program that targeted online sexual predators in Operation Safe Summer. In the years since then, he'd built a national reputation based on trolling for internet predators, engaging them online, then providing them opportunities to commit just enough acts to justify criminal attempt charges. Like most criminal prosecutions, most defendants and their cases settled instead of risking a serious conviction at trial.

Now, with years of experience under his belt, Spector was part of the elite multi-agency Law Enforcement Against Child Harm (LEACH) Task Force, a team of determined, dedicated officers specializing in protecting children from predators on the internet and in real life.

Just as sexual predators know exactly how to approach their victims, so Spector was a master of ferreting out what the predators wanted and mirroring their behaviors. For Spector, there was something exquisitely right about finding an adult who was lying to children to entice them into sexual activity and using their own tactics against them. Few escaped once Spector targeted them. He was proud of his work, with good reason. He enjoyed it. It would be fair to say that he got off on it.

On Monday afternoon, May 12, Spector was working a familiar hunting ground, AOL's FamLuv chat room. FamLuv was known to law enforcement as a clearing-house for downloading and trading child porn and a gathering spot for a small subset of men seeking contact sex with children.

Spector was a regular in FamLuv. He used the screen

name *TravinDadFl* and called himself "Wayne" in private chats.

Three years prior, "Wayne" had built the case that had led to the conviction of a Lakeland, Florida, businessman named Robert Collins Latham. Fifty-year-old Latham was the child predator every parent dreads. At the time of his arrest—en route to what he believed would be sex in a Tampa hotel room with an eleven-year-old child—Latham was president of Lakeland City Baseball, a youth organization that sponsors Little League teams.

Spector watched the comments and questions scroll by, the odd abbreviations and proliferation of ellipses a familiar second language. He made an occasional comment, baiting the hook and leaving it dangling, trolling for a bite. It was a sordid yet delicate business, fishing for pedophiles, walking a thin line between providing an opportunity and out and out entrapment.

Initially, Stan Rothenberg was no different than any other pervert he'd stalked in the steamier corners of AOL chat rooms. Developing the relationship had taken time, but Spector was an old hand at it. Years of experience and a bright, inquisitive mind had honed his ability to take on another persona.

■ ■ ■

At 4:38 p.m. that Monday, Spector was pinged by an AOL user announcing himself as *LuvYngBButts*. After a few exchanges, the man—Spector had no reason to doubt it was a man—typed that he lived in Fort Lauderdale. The two exchanged a brief, sexually-explicit series of instant messages.

LuvYngBButts was interested in "dad/son and dad/ dau activity." Written in the ungrammatical shorthand— abbreviations, misspellings, ellipsis—typical of online chatter, these messages were obscene, perhaps erotic in themselves.

Like all hunters, Spector experienced a tingle of excitement at the first scent of his prey. Now, traps had to be laid, bait proffered, all while steering—arguably, at least— clear of the slightest hint of entrapment. *Providing an opportunity* for a pervert to commit a criminal act was one thing. Instigating it was an entirely different matter. Cross over that line, and every bit of evidence that Spector gathered would come back to bite him as support for a defense of entrapment.

Opportunity, Spector reminded himself. *Just opportunity. Let the pervert take the next step.*

Spector: *What ages u into?*

Rothenberg: *Prob 8-plus, but open...*

Spector: *What were you really looking for?*

Rothenberg: *Meeting dad with son/dau and group activity.*

Spector indicates he was sexually involved with his daughter.

Rothenberg: *It was a total turn on for me to watch a dad fuckin his dau (or asking me to get involved too)*

Rothenberg: *I haven't had any real time sex with below 18 male or f.*

Spector: *So just fantasy for you?*

Rothenberg: *Up until now. . . Do you share your dau with any buds?*

Spector responded he had "previously shared his daughter."

■ ■ ■

Stan leaned back in his chair and felt of flutter of excitement tinged with fear. Could he go through with it? The man he'd been chatting with sounded exceptionally sexy. Could this be what Stan had been looking for?

The new had worn off of typing and chatting and talking dirty online. Stan was ready to take it to the next level, to get back that gut-deep thrill and arousal that the chat rooms had first given him. What Stan wanted, and what he intended to get, was to hook up with this sexy dad and take "pervy talk" to a whole new level—in person, instead of online.

Hesitantly, Stan typed his phone number into the instant message to *TravinDadFl.*

■ ■ ■

Their first phone call went well. In their brief, staccato exchanges, Stanley pressed "Wayne" for details about his sexual encounters with his eleven-year-old daughter.

"Wayne" complied, then drew Stan out, asking Stan if he wanted to be part of the action. Stan said he was willing. "Wayne" said he lived about one hundred miles north of Fort Lauderdale. The two agreed to meet in Port St. Lucie on Friday, May 16.

When Stan hung up from talking to "Wayne," Stan was more excited than he'd been in months.

Despite his arousal, Stan could feel his anxiety battering at the hatches. There was a child involved, a girl. What would he do? Watch? Take part? What *could* he do? Repulsed sexually by females, suffering from anxiety attacks and erectile dysfunction, Stan was not interested in "doing" anything.

But to get "Wayne" to talk dirty, he'd told "Wayne" he was willing. And to prove it to "Wayne," he'd called a cheap motel in Fort Pierce and reserved a room.

Surely it wasn't a set up. He'd asked Wayne straight out if he were a cop, and Wayne had been equally worried about Stan being a cop.

No, it was safe. It wasn't just a hook up.

It was a friendship.

Wayne himself had said so.

Spector:	*And, you know, I hope we can maybe grab some dinner or something afterwards. I mean I hope, you know, I hate to sound, you know. I want this to be a relationship because we're all, I don't want it to be, you know what I mean?*
Rothenberg:	*Right.*

Spector: *A friendship. You know. I'd like it to be a friendship as well. We're—*

Rothenberg: *Right.*

Spector: *You know. This isn't just a one-time thing.*

Rothenberg: *Right. Right. Okay. I'm with you on that.*

Spector: *Okay, good.*

Rothenberg: *And, I'm probably going to be a lot more nervous than you.*

Spector: *Well, I'm nervous too, believe me. That's why I asked you probably ahalfofdozen times.x [Laughing]*

Rothenberg: *Well, you're going to have to help me out, so, uh, you know. I, I, I think once, that's why, I, you know when you said oh; I like to talk to people, you know, on the phone and get to know. I'm the, I'm the same way, you know.*

Spector: *Um, good.*

Rothenberg: *I mean, its such an unusual occurrence for me to run into somebody like you and be invited—*

Spector: *Ditto.*

Rothenberg: *—I mean, I can tell you, it doesn't happen. Most people, they were bullshitters.*

Spector: *Right. Well, I hope you don't think I'm a bullshitter.*

Rothenberg: *No, not at all. Not at all. I mean, its, I have to admit, I am taking back by the, by the, I'm taken, I feel, I feel honored that you're willing to have me and it was a little bit hard for me to right now internally accept the fact that hey this, this, this was going to happen. You know, hopefully. And, I mean its like wow.*

Then the unexpected happened: Stan's psychologist called to cancel their 3 p.m. appointment on May 13. All at once the fantasy encounter became insanely close to becoming reality. It was exciting beyond measure. It was going to happen. He could still feel excited, aroused, human, alive!

At 10:57 a.m. Stan typed:

Good Morning. My afternoon 3 PM appointment had been changed, so I'd feel so much better if I could take a drive up to meet you (can be at your place, McDonald's, Dunkin' Donuts, etc.) and just feel better about everything.
Call me on my cell when u get this message.
Stanley.

Then Stan stepped away from his computer, mind reeling with adrenalin. He showered, shaved, and then pulled on his favorite pair of khaki shorts and a short-sleeve knit pullover. He was no longer a sixty-four-year-old geezer, but a teenager on a big date. He felt giddy with anticipation. At the last moment, to keep the anxiety at bay so he could hold on to the feeling, he swallowed his morning Klonopin, two milligrams.

Later, much later, Stan would repeatedly make it clear that he'd told Spector to come alone, that no children were to be involved. Those comments were not reflected in Spector's affidavit.

■ ■ ■

As Stan headed out the door, he glanced around his 2,500-square foot, tastefully furnished condominium and beyond to the restless ocean. Clouds had rolled in, turning the turquoise ocean to slate gray. David had painted so many of the outsized paintings covering the walls. They were the last physical links Stan had to David and the secure, stable life they'd planned together.

But David was gone. Like it or not, this would have to do.

First date jitters. David would have known what to do. Stan could feel the anxiety hovering at the edges of his mind, kept only partially at bay by the Klonopin.

A gift, a small token. That's what you do on a first date. This had to be right; everything had to be perfect.

Flowers? No. Too impractical for the drive up there, and he had no idea what kind of flowers "Wayne" liked, if he liked them at all.

So what do you take a child molester instead of flowers or candy?

It came to him almost instantly. He was going to meet

a self-confessed child molester, one who supposedly abused his own daughter.

Stan smiled. He had just the thing.

Instead of flowers, you take a flash drive stuffed with child porn pictures.

Just before he left, Stan made what would be his last good decision for many years to come. Rather than take the thumb drive of porn with him, he left it at his condo, tucked under his mattress.

Three

AN HOUR AND a half later, Stanley Rothenberg's dreams came crashing down on him. He'd ignored the hot, steaming asphalt surrounding the fast food joint, the smell of French fries, and the screaming toddlers. He saw the crowds of families, heard the screaming children and parents correcting them in myriad foreign languages. Even the cheesy little white rental car, reeking of commercial sanitizer and multiple owners, hadn't completely hit him.

But when he saw "Wayne," it all hit him at once. A deep sense of dismay swept through him, completely driving out the eager anticipation that had filled him for the last week. "Wayne" was nothing like the hot, steamy hunk that Stan had expected. Even though "Wayne" had repeatedly said that he was a straight guy and that there was no chance that Rothenberg and "Wayne" would get together, Stan had somehow held out some hope. Still, even if that didn't happen, at least he would get to talk dirty face to face with a really hot guy. That was his only goal.

Now, faced with a short, fat, balding man who looked more like an accountant than anything else, Rothenberg was totally nonplussed. The two men greeted each other, and Stan felt the normal benzodiazepine-induced fog roll back over him. He slipped out of anticipation and was operating on autopilot.

To give himself a few moments to come to terms with this new reality, he suggested that they get some coffee. They walked into the fast food store, got coffee, and returned to the rental car.

"My mind was on complete autopilot the entire time in his car," Stan said later. "I wasn't enamored with the dad's looks, but I'd taken the time to drive up there, so I figured I might as well complete my mission. I'm trying to get to dirty talk—to chat with a no-limits boundary. I've often done this on the phone, but never person-to-person. The newness of it really grabs me."

But this—this was not what he imagined at all. Sitting in the cramped confines of a compact rental car—Stan was significantly taller than six feet—with a balding gnome next to him.

"I do remember becoming bored," Stan said. "I did ask why he was driving a rental car. It didn't take me long. I found him uninteresting. I wanted to get out of the car and go home. I had an affair to attend in Fort Lauderdale that night."

From the moment he pulled into the parking lot, Stan had been approaching the edge of a cliff. Behind him, the vast machinery of the criminal justice system was creeping forward, herding him toward the edge. Stan had no idea how much danger he was in.

■ ■ ■

Women and toddlers clutching takeout bags stared aghast as Stan was jerked out of the car, handcuffed, and stuffed into a police car.

Stan was transported to St. Lucie County Jail. There, he was read his Miranda rights. He declined to make any statement or answer any questions, not out of caution and a desire for counsel, but because he could simply form no words other than his name and address.

Things like this didn't happen to Stanley G. Rothenberg. This had to be a terrible mistake of some sort. He'd talk to the detectives and get it all cleared up just as soon as he got control of his words. He'd explain it all to them; they'd understand; they'd let him go.

Dazed, confused, and paralyzed with dread, Stan was booked and tossed into the holding cell with the usual assortment of accused drug dealers, muggers, petty thieves, wife beaters, and drunks who populate jails.

It seemed so obvious it was a mistake that Stan fastened onto odd, unrelated, and trivial alarms. He worried about his car, what would happen to it being left in the fast food parking lot. He worried about being late for an award being presented to his lover, Ron, for community service.

He disconnected. All of it was happening to someone else.

■ ■ ■

Stan might not have believed it was happening, but Spector did. As out of his element as Stan was, Spector was the opposite. The detective immediately contacted Fort

Lauderdale detective John Jensen and told Jensen that
Rothenberg was in custody. He faxed Jensen a probable
cause affidavit to serve as the basis for Jensen getting a
search warrant.

According to Detective Spector's Affidavit:

> *On May 13, 2008, the undercover contacted Fort Lau-
> derdale Police Detective John Jensen and requested
> his assistance. The undercover sent Detective Jensen
> his probable cause affidavit and requested he
> obtain a search warrant for Rothenberg's Fort
> Lauderdale residence. Detective Jensen obtained
> and served the search warrant later that evening.
> Detective Jensen indicated he found a thumbnail
> drive under a bed mattress in Rothenberg's bedroom,
> along with a laptop computer. Detective Jensen fur-
> ther stated he found numerous printed computer chats,
> including chats with the undercover, in Rothen-
> berg's bedroom. Detective Jensen stated some of the
> chats appeared to be individuals communicating
> about incest.*

Stanley's astounded partner, Ron, had been trying to
track down Stan all day, and when Jensen showed up, Ron
was immediately convinced Rothenberg had been in a terrible car accident or taken ill.

Ron knew nothing about Stan's online life, and certainly not about the FamLuv chatroom, and there was
no evidence to charge him with any related offense. Even
though he'd committed no crime, the comfortable life Ron
had known was about to disappear.

The search immediately yielded the thumb drive Rothenberg mentioned. It was under the mattress in Rothenberg's

bedroom, just where he said it was. He and his lover, Ron, slept in separate rooms.

Jensen confiscated the Toshiba laptop. Later, a forensics examination would reveal numerous images of child pornography. He also carried off a box of computer printouts—Stanley's chats, including the recent instant messages between *LuvYngBButts* and "Wayne."

Why keep transcripts of the chats?

Rothenberg—computer illiterate—printed them out so he could keep his stories straight. He had too many story lines going with too many families, and given his benzodiazepine addiction, his short-term memory was shot. He printed them out so he could enjoy them later and keep track of the men he was talking to. The overwhelming percentage of his dirty talk chats were purely homosexual.

But two chat transcripts out of the boxes seized were different. Just two, a miniscule percentage.

Those two brief chats would be a critical part of the case against Stan. Prosecutors would use them to establish a "pattern of criminal behavior."

■ ■ ■

Back in jail, Stan finally calmed down enough to think through his situation. He was convinced that he could clear it all up by talking to the detectives, explaining what seemed obvious to him. He'd confirm what they already knew—no point in denying that he had the thumb drive with the child porn on it or that he'd driven up to have a "talk dirty" session with Wayne. Once they saw he was being straight up with them, they'd believe him and let him go.

It seemed completely obvious to Stan. After all, it wasn't like he'd ever even been seen in public with someone like Spector.

At the jail, Stan's meltdown was complete. According to court transcripts, rather than demanding a lawyer, Rothenberg "re-initiates contact with Detective Spector. At that time, the defendant provided a full taped confession."

Stan thought this was ludicrous. All he'd done was confirm what they already knew. In his words, "those were all things that they knew to be facts anyway or that they already had in their possession." He could not see the harm in telling them what they already knew. In his mind, that would clear everything up, and he'd be allowed to go home.

But how could he provide a full confession to something he never intended to do? In fact, that something that was completely factually impossible, since there was no child.

■ ■ ■

On Monday, Stanley Rothenberg had gone to bed in a luxury condo with the starlit Atlantic gleaming beyond his window. On Tuesday, he'd been stripped of his wallet, cell phone, and gold chain, fingerprinted, processed, and handed an orange jumpsuit. He was locked in a cell in a two-tier pod containing twenty-four other cells. Two, sometimes three, men crowded in each cell. The third man in each cell slept with his possessions in a concrete tub cemented to the center of the floor.

It seemed like no time at all before he was booked and arraigned via video conference. By then, the walls were starting to close in on him.

At 8:00 that night, he made his first collect phone calls. The first one was to Ron Duron, who told him about the search and seizure and warrant. By then, after having been exposed to the worst the city had to offer in the holding cell, Stan started to realize he need the best outside help he could get. It still seemed ludicrous that they hadn't let him go once he'd explained what happened.

Spector called the taped statement Rothenberg made "a confession."

From Spector's deposition: "The Suspect said he wanted to 'fuck' the undercover's daughter . . . he wanted to give the undercover's daughter 'oral sex' . . . He had images on a thumbnail (sic) of children ages six to seventeen. He was going to bring the thumbnail drive on Friday when he travels . . . to meet the undercover and his daughter."

Stan knew it was just a statement of facts. How can they not see that? Even Spector admitted that wasn't the "entire portion" of the meeting. Spector left out everything that put that statement into context for what it was— talking dirty on the internet.

■ ■ ■

On Wednesday morning, Stan finally reached out to his family. He called his younger brother, Gil Rothenberg, who was a high-level Department of Justice official in Washington, D.C. It wasn't a pleasant conversation.

But family was family, and whatever his feelings were about Stan and his arrest, Gil agreed to help. He did some research and found former Assistant US Attorney (AUSA) Edward Page, a defense attorney.

Gil set up a conference call, and the three of them discussed what would happen next. Page went over the basics: bail, trial scheduling, potential defenses, possible pleadings. To Stan, it was like learning to speak a new and foreign language.

But to Stan's relief, Page sounded like he spoke this new language fluently. Finally, Stan had someone on his side, someone who would listen to what he'd been trying to explain since the moment he'd been arrested.

As bad as the charges were, Stan had a bigger and more immediate problem: the imminent benzodiazepine withdrawal he was about to undergo.

Stan was on two milligrams of Klonopin twice a day. Without it, he would go into serious withdrawal. At that moment, at that time, avoiding withdrawal was more important to him than any discussion of procedures or plea agreements.

If Stan had been charged with profiteering, tax fraud, or any other sort of white-collar crime, Edward Page would have been an excellent choice. He was an experienced attorney, well-versed in dealing with white-collar crime, and a veteran of the federal prosecution system.

But it wasn't a white-collar crime. It was a child molestation case with tough facts made even worse by the details Spector invented. It took a certain kind of experience to understand the wide range of sexual behavior and compare that with what the law deems a crime.

Unfortunately, Edward Page would not be the only lawyer to cringe at the facts of the charges.

Just why did Stan say what he said, do what he did? Why would he talk like that if he didn't intend to have sex with a child?

"It was very difficult, if not impossible to precisely extrapolate why I did what I did," Stan said. "The human mind is extremely complicated when it comes to sex. There were multiple nuances and unconscious thoughts that took place at lightning speed. Specific words or behaviors by the undercover cop could have encouraged me to continue on with our McDonald's parking lot chat."

■ ■ ■

A few days later, a state grand jury indicted Rothenberg on two felony counts. The judge set bail at $250,000.

Page advised against posting bond. Stan was flabbergasted, but Page told him the Department of Justice was taking over the prosecution.

That was the worst possible news. The Feds didn't prosecute until they were certain they could get a conviction and their conviction rates consistently topped 95 percent. The government was going to make an example out of this successful man who happened to be gay.

If convicted on both counts, Stan would face "10 to life" on one felony count.

"There was absolutely no way that my behavior could possibly net me such a horrendous prison term," Rothenberg insisted in 2016. "It defies logic. It defies common sense. It defies reality." He remembered the following from that meeting:

Rothenberg: *Can I plead insanity?*

Page: *That won't fly.*

Rothenberg: *How can I prove I'm innocent?*

Page: *You can prove you had no intention of having sex with that fictitious girl.*

Four

IN THE SPRING of 2008, the highly-publicized Operation Safe Summer sting operations snared twenty-seven alleged pedophiles and collectors and dealers of child pornography. Overwhelmingly, they were internet stings—set up by undercover cops prowling bulletin boards and chat rooms—part of an effort the US Department of Justice funded around the country.

Neil Spector personally bagged many of the miscreants. In one instance, he portrayed himself as a father who offered his eleven-year-old daughter to a fisherman in exchange for diving lessons and a sack of spiny lobsters.

Stanley Rothenberg stood out among the accused. He was the oldest by many years. Well-educated and affluent, he had a very successful business career highlighted by a history of volunteerism and community service. He was homosexual—openly gay, exclusively gay.

"I can't stand the thought of sex with an adult female,

much less an eleven-year-old girl who's supposedly hand-icapped!" Rothenberg insisted.

Stan grew up during an era where children simply did not register with most gay men. According to his sister and brother-in-law, Rothenberg didn't particularly like children. Stanley was the uncle guaranteed not to show up at the kids' birthday parties.

Fred Halper, who worked with Rothenberg fifty years ago and has remained a close friend, insisted, "Stan was never, ever interested in females, especially young females. I believe he was drawn in by this policeman, the detective. He was probably fascinated by a man who was having sex with his own daughter."

Anthropologist Douglas Feldman had been a friend of Stan's for nearly two decades. The two traveled together, and had gone to the beach, bars, and even a gay syna-gogue together.

"Never once during the entire time, did Stan ever express any sexual interest in children," Feldman said. "Now for the real shocker: never once did he express any interest in females. When I heard he'd been arrested going after a female, I said, 'Something was really wrong with this picture!'"

Feldman was so sure of this, he'd be comfortable having Rothenberg babysitting his nieces and nephews. "I'd have no qualms whatsoever."

Jerry Effron, another old friend, agreed: "I'd trust him without hesitation."

■ ■ ■

Out of the closet since he was in his twenties, Rothenberg spent his adult life living with his partner in an exquisitely restored home in Richmond. Their life together was a swirl of cocktail parties and charitable benefits, gay fundraisers, cruises, and overseas travel, rounded always by hard work and entrepreneurialism.

And then David died.

He tried to continue that lifestyle after he moved to Fort Lauderdale in 1997, but by then he was fifty-three years old, past his prime in a gay culture where youth and beauty were paramount. His new lover, Ron, possessed these attributes, but the two drew apart. Rothenberg said they were "sexually and emotionally incompatible."

By 2008, Stan was bored, horny, thrill-seeking, and living on little more than fantasies.

Did he truly desire to have sex with a handicapped child as Detective Spector alleges?

It was very unlikely, given his character, history, and the evidence. Detective Spector's own deposition accurately described Rothenberg's state of mind at the moment of his arrest: "However, the defendant indicated he was not sure if he actually would have had sex with the child."

■ ■ ■

That first night, Stan lay sleepless, thrashing on a plastic mattress on a concrete shelf protruding from the back wall of a cell. He shivered under a thin blanket because jailers keep thermostats at near-frigid levels to suppress the germs, stench, and desires of men crowded together in small spaces.

At 4:30 a.m., overhead lights hummed to life. Electronic locks snapped open. Breakfast time.

Stan shuffled to the front of the pod where he was handed plastic utensils and a tray of tasteless food. After the meal, he and the other prisoners tramped back to the cells. The locks snapped closed. The lights dimmed. Most of the men went back to sleep. Stan was not among them.

■　■　■

Days passed. The trauma of the arrest was compounded by a debilitating slide into drug withdrawal.

Klonopin (clonazepam) is a powerful antianxiety medication originally developed to suppress epileptic seizures. Like its sister drugs—Valium, Xanax, and Ativan—it is a benzodiazepine (benzo in street jargon), highly addictive, rife with side effects, notoriously difficult to kick.

Stan knew how bad it was going to be, and that dread kept him constantly agitated. In the 1990s and early 2000s, he checked himself into mental hospitals and rehab facilities on five different occasions, trying to break a thirty-year dependency. Each time he came away defeated and feeling "like I was about to die."

There's no doubt that withdrawal from benzos can kill. In 1986, Stevie Nicks, lead singer for the rock group, Fleetwood Mac, was prescribed Klonopin while undergoing treatment for cocaine addiction at the Betty Ford Center. She developed a benzodiazepine dependency. This second addiction to a horrible, dangerous drug led to another seven-week hospitalization. As Nicks recalled, "It was like somebody opened up a door and pushed me into hell."

Rothenberg began to suffer acute physical pain (muscle aches, cramps, severe anxiety, short-term memory loss, and disorientation) as well as devastating psychological effects associated with withdrawing cold turkey. At the same time, he was trying to come to terms with the astounding notion that he was facing life in prison.

Suicide soon seemed a plausible alternative.

That's not an uncommon conclusion for people withdrawing from benzos. In 1996, actress Margaux Hemingway committed suicide by overdosing on a barbiturate-benzodiazepine cocktail. Hollywood producer Don Simpson's (*Beverly Hills Cop*) death had been linked to a benzodiazepine overdose. Klonopin was one of the drugs detected during an autopsy of *Playboy* centerfold Anna Nicole Smith who overdosed in 2007. Novelist David Foster Wallace, considered by many the literary voice of his generation, was prescribed Klonopin to help alleviate a profound depression. He later hung himself. Stevie Nicks described a "devastating loss of creativity," as the worst effect of Klonopin.

"The fabulous Stevie everyone knew just disappeared," she told a reporter. "I became what I call 'the Whatever Person.' I didn't care about anything."

Decades of benzodiazepine abuse damaged and desensitized Stanley Rothenberg to the point where, desperate for stimulation and excitement, he roamed the dark rooms of the internet heedless of behavior or consequence. In short, he was mentally ill, incapacitated, and lacked the will, the awareness, and the strength to pull back from destructive behavior.

Did that constitute insanity? Or at least diminished capacity? Under the siege of benzo withdrawal, Stan's mind was no longer under his complete control. He was absolutely incompetent to make many of the decisions he would soon face.

■ ■ ■

Stan was transferred to the jail's basement infirmary where he immediately encountered the classic catch–22 of withdrawal in jail. Everyone acknowledged he was sick because he was withdrawing from his prescription medication, but everything he was on was red-flagged as an abuse drug. The end result was he was not given anything.

"The infirmary was a hellhole," Stan recalled. "I'm locked in a small cell with two other men. We sit and sleep in hard plastic boats. We're issued one sheet, no pillow, nothing else but a metal toilet and sink, and a small shower stall. The boats fill every square inch of floor space. There was no room to walk around or even stretch. Three sardines in a can. This was the infirmary! And yes, the jail's psychiatrist had zero compassion."

Two months later, on July 10, Ed Page filed an emergency medication motion requiring the US Marshals Service and the St. Lucie County Jail "to provide previously prescribed medication." The motion covered Klonopin and three other prescription drugs Stan was taking at the time of his arrest: Lyrica (for neuropathy), Acyclovir (an antiviral used to treat cold sores and herpes infections), and Ditropan (for overactive bladder).

At the hearing on the motion, Stan described his deteriorating physical health. Stan took the stand and testified under oath, "I am in agony." On July 20, Magistrate Judge Frank J. Lynch Jr. denied the motion.

Stan complained to one of the prisoners in his pod.

"A Jewish guy," he recalled, "who tells me about the best attorney in the world."

This modern-day Brandeis was supposedly able to

engineer huge reductions in inmates' sentences by arguing a "learning disability." The man was Michael Metz.

"I want to believe that Metz would work wonders for me too," Stan said.

■ ■ ■

Stan fired Ed Page. He hired West Palm Beach law firm Lubin & Metz. West Palm Beach was just a short hour's drive from Port St. Lucie, an added benefit Stan assured himself.

"But when Michael Metz shows up, I'm in horrible benzo withdrawal," Stan recalled. "I don't even know what day or month it is. I'm so sick I can barely hold a rational conversation. Michael's fee was $100,000 up front. No matter if I go to trial or not.

"What could I do? I'm in handcuffs. I'm in withdrawal. I'm facing life in prison. I have no way of even making an unmonitored phone call. I tell Metz I need to talk to Ron (Duron) about getting the money. I have a General American life insurance policy with a death benefit of $600,000. I cash it in for $125,000. I get the money, but really, it was just another nail in my coffin.

"When Metz and his partner, Richard Lubin, bring a contract for me to sign. I've slept less than three hours a night for weeks. I can't focus enough to see or read anything. I look near death. The only thing I can think about was getting out of this jail. I sign on the dotted line and plead with them to get me out before I die."

Metz moved quickly. As an excellent and experienced criminal defense attorney, he knew how the system worked. He contacted the US Marshal (responsible for federal prisoners held in county jails) and arranged

for Stan to be transferred to the nearby Palm Beach
County Jail.

On July 10, 2008, Metz filed a MOTION TO REQUIRE THE
UNITED STATES MARSHALS SERVICE AND THE ST. LUCIE
COUNTY JAIL TO PROVIDE PREVIOUSLY PRESCRIBED MED-
ICATION, asking the Court "… pursuant to Fed.R.Crim.P.
47, to enter an order requiring that the United States Marshals Service and the West Palm Beach County Jail to
provide to Rothenberg with Clonazepam or another drug
such as Zyprexa that would provide him relief from his
anxiety disorder …."

To a desperate man, that alone was a huge victory.

■ ■ ■

The West Palm Beach County Jail was a sunlit, elev-
en-story high-rise edged by palm trees and a portico. It
looked like one of the Hampton Inns dotting the I-95 corridor. Compared with the St. Lucie County Jail, West Palm
Beach seemed, at first glance, a resort. Stan was assigned
to a single-man cell on the ninth floor.

"I can look through windows and see outside," he
recalled. "The staff seems attentive. I begin to feel human."

After a few days, he reported to Sick Call, shuffling
along the corridors with a host of other prisoners. He took
a seat and watched the hours on the wall clock tick slowly
away. At some point, a trustee announced his name.

"I jump to attention and move to a smaller waiting
room. Two minutes later, the doctor, a psychiatrist, calls
me by name. I enter his office and sit down. I feel my eyes
tearing up as he shuffles his papers. I break down. I'm no
longer able to contain all this pain."

Stan's words poured out disjointed, fragmented bits of

personal history—an uncertain and often unhappy child-hood; an adolescence defined, as it was for so many gay men, by shame, confusion, and longing; the happiness and success he'd had after meeting David, his life partner; the long journey into the dark night of grief and addiction; the chat rooms, his entrapment and arrest; the shame, followed by the months isolated and misunderstood in a jail packed with criminals; his worsening anxiety and pain—all compounded by the devastating, life-draining withdrawal.

"The doctor speaks with some compassion," Stan recalled. "He seems familiar with benzodiazepine withdrawal. He jots some notes and assures me he'll reinstate my Klonopin but at half my former dosage. I'd have to wait until morning for the requisition to be processed. I've just got to hold on for fourteen more hours."

In a few days, the world began to right itself. The medication cut his withdrawal symptoms in half. Stan could move around, engage with other inmates, speak rationally with Michael Metz, and communicate by phone and mail with his extensive circle of friends and family.

Some would stay loyal to him in the long years ahead. Others would not.

Five

2008
Fort Lauderdale, Florida

STAN SPENT THE summer convincing himself and anyone who would listen that it was all a mistake, a miscarriage of justice, an enormous overreaction, a nightmare from which he would soon be set free. He was convinced that if he could just get someone in authority to listen to him, they'd understand immediately and release him.

He kept repeating that he was sorry, ready to make amends, didn't fully understand the gravity of the situation he created. He pointed out that he was lost in a benzodiazepine fog at the time it all happened and that his ability to make reasoned judgments was impaired. He was willing to accept a punishment suitable to his crime which, he reasoned, was a sin of omission—shameful words and images floating in the ether—not a sin of commission. He never touched anyone, nor would he ever touch a child sexually.

Nobody was listening. The world was preoccupied with other events. A junior senator from Illinois, Barack Obama, was mounting a historic run for the White House.

On Wall Street, the financial markets were months from the meltdown that would send the American economy reeling for almost a decade. The endless ground wars raging in Iraq and Afghanistan were crossing borders, bleeding into Pakistan, Syria, and Turkey, edging closer to the democracies of the West.

Americans were struggling with post–9/11 malaise, now metastasized and grown amorphous. Fear was in the air. The world was a riskier place. This was not the same unease felt during the Cold War—the unpleasant assurance that any havoc the Soviets created would be offset by the certainty of mutual assured destruction.

This was new risk, an asymmetric risk—threats posed by unsuspected people in unimagined places, at unforeseen times. It was risk enhanced by anonymity, by predators assuming multiple identities, entering homes, and breeching boundaries with the ease of a keyboard click. In America, the front line of this troubling war was cyberspace.

The internet brought the bogeyman into people's homes. No longer was it a person lurking around a playground or a church, someone who alert parents could watch out for. Now the monster was no longer climbing in through bedroom windows but slipping easily into their children's bedrooms through the internet.

Monsters like Stanley Rothenberg. He was the fiend who forced impoverished Third World children into slavery and sexual abominations. He was the molester. He was the sum of all fears.

The fact that none of that was even remotely true didn't matter.

■ ■ ■

Michael Metz arrived and advised Stan that the federal government would definitely be prosecuting him. The US Attorney was preparing to charge him with "Using a computer in interstate commerce to knowingly attempt to induce an individual under eighteen to engage in criminal sexual activity," a felony that carried a mandatory minimum sentence of ten years and up to life in prison. He would also face a second felony count carrying a sentence of up to ten years for, "Knowingly possessing one or more visual depictions transmitted in interstate commerce by computer involving a minor engaging in sexually explicit conduct."

The jailhouse lawyers all around Stan warned him that federal prosecutors handpicked slam-dunk prosecutions to up their conviction rates to astronomical levels. To continue the unfortunate image, Stan was either a basketball about to be jammed into a net or a backboard about to be shattered into a thousand pieces.

"I was dumbfounded," Stan recalled. "Stupefied. Speechless. Could a few online chats and phone calls end up landing me in prison for life? I was so frightened, so unable to comprehend what was happening, that I began to lose touch with reality."

Metz left Stan to stumble back to his cell. The next days passed in a blur. Still in acute benzo withdrawal, Stan vaguely remembers walking round and round the pod's second-floor balcony—crying, swearing, pleading, beseeching the heavens: "This can't be happening to me," he repeated over and over.

No one listened. No one answered.

■ ■ ■

In 1998, the Department of Justice created the Internet Crimes Against Children Task Force (ICAC) to equip state and local law enforcement agencies with the manpower and technology to go after online users and distributors of child pornography. New federal laws were passed to make prosecuting easier and to extend the sentences of so-called noncontact sex offenders lurking in chat rooms and frequenting online bulletin boards such as the *Cache*, a virtual trading post containing hundreds of thousands of child porn images. Many states followed the fed's lead, enacting or dramatically toughening laws targeting internet criminals. Like the old Wild West, the new digital frontier demanded aggressive lawmen like Wyatt Earp and Pat Garrett. In South Florida, Neil Spector rode into town.

No one paid much attention to the actual facts. Statistics developed by the Department of Justice and the National Center for Missing and Exploited Children (NCMEC) indicate that most child homicides and 30 percent of sexual assaults on children were committed by family members. Research into pedophilia suggests it may be genetic—that most men who download and view child porn were unlikely to molest a flesh-and-blood child. No matter, well-intended policymaking became blatant overreaction.

Stan had never heard of Operation Safe Summer, Megan's Law, or Adam Walsh. He couldn't identify NCMEC, and certainly not the myriad law enforcement entities massing to eradicate this imagined army of pedophiles.

Understanding the entire industry devoted to finding

and prosecuting child molesters was beyond him. Stan had terrible difficulty processing and collating information, connecting disparate thoughts, distilling cause and effect. He had had this problem his entire life, to the point where he had coined a term for it, one clearly missing from the bible of psychopathology, the *Diagnostic and Statistical Manual of Mental Disorders* (DSM). He named his disability "blocking."

In his mind, these sweeping developments in society, law enforcement, and information technology boiled down to a nagging unease about talking dirty and being caught up in a police sting operation. Stanley Rothenberg was a voyeur trafficking in other people's fantasies—not so much a criminal as a sexually frustrated old man.

But now, under the new legislation, a criminal.

■ ■ ■

Stan may have been frozen in time, but the new, disruptive technologies like email and e-commerce triggered dramatic changes in the way people worked, did business, found pleasure, and lived their lives. Stan was bored, lustful, and backward-looking, but around him, things were happening faster and faster like the fluttering pages of calendars showing the passing of time. Sometimes, it felt as if time itself had been compressed, and what joy he'd known had retreated into the distant past.

"How did my life pass so quickly?" he wondered, a refrain familiar to every middle-aged man. With too much time on his hands and too few interests, Stan had gone surfing on the wave of the Information Age, searching for something—anything—to break through the benzo haze.

■ ■ ■

Late in May, Stan appeared before Magistrate Judge Edward Lynch to be arraigned on the two felony charges. The prosecutor, a tough, young Assistant US Attorney named Rinku Talwar, outlined the government's case against him. Given the evidence and the new statutes, Rinku thought a conviction was a slam dunk. She opposed the motion to grant bail.

"Already I was underwater," Stan remembered. Nonetheless, he entered a plea of not guilty. And with that plea, Stan was officially awaiting trial.

Federal law, codified at 18 USC sec. 3142 provides:

(a)In General.—Upon the appearance before a judicial officer of a person charged with an offense, the judicial officer shall issue an order that, pending trial, the person be—

(1) released on personal recognizance or upon execution of an unsecured appearance bond, under subsection (b) of this section;

(2) released on a condition or combination of conditions under subsection (c) of this section;

(3) temporarily detained to permit revocation of conditional release, deportation, or exclusion under subsection (d) of this section; or

(4) detained under subsection (e) of this section.

On the face of it, Stan was a good prospect for bail. Stan had never been in trouble with the law in his life. He was a property owner, had substantial assets, was actively engaged in volunteerism in his community, and was certainly no flight risk—all good arguments for granting bail.

But the law was against him. Subsection e(3) says:

Subject to rebuttal by the person, it shall be presumed

that no condition or combination of conditions will reasonably assure the appearance of the person as required and the safety of the community if the judicial officer finds that there is probable cause to believe that the person committed—

(A) an offense for which a maximum term of imprisonment of ten years or more is prescribed in the Controlled Substances Act (21 USC 801 et seq.), the Controlled Substances Import and Export Act (21 USC 951 et seq.), or chapter 705 of title 46;

(B) an offense under section 924(c), 956(a), or 2332b of this title;

(C) an offense listed in section 2332b(g)(5)(B) of title 18, United States Code, for which a maximum term of imprisonment of 10 years or more is prescribed;

(D) an offense under chapter 77 of this title for which a maximum term of imprisonment of 20 years or more is prescribed;

On May 30, 2008, Judge Lynch ordered Stan "Detained prior to trial and the conclusion thereof."

"If I'd gotten out on bail," Stan said wistfully, "I would have hired a different attorney. I would have gotten advice from my siblings. I would have been more in control of the benzo mess. At least I would have the benefit of being free while of all this was ongoing. Not getting bail killed me. I lost the balance in my life because a magistrate judge apparently felt that giving me home confinement with an ankle monitor was not keeping America safe enough. He just had to keep me locked up. Was this the best a federal judge could have done?"

One veteran criminal attorney familiar with the case shrugged. "Really, who's going to grant bail to a child molester?"

The actual wording of the order denying Stan bail foreshadowed what was ahead: "The Court found that no condition or combination of conditions will reasonably assure the safety of any other person and the community."

"Am I really the monster of all monsters?" Stan wondered as he was led away in shackles.

Six

THE ROTHENBERG HOME sprawled across a desirable corner lot in Richmond's West End. White clapboards and green shutters, the very epitome of Southern grace, housed Stan and his four siblings. For Joe Rothenberg, everything about the house screamed success. Stan's father, one of ten children, luxuriated in the space, felt it was validation of everything he'd done. He may have lived in cramped quarters as a child, but his children would have better by dint of hard work and education. For a Jew in Richmond in the 1950s, West End was as upwardly mobile as it got.

The affluent populations of Richmond led parallel lives stratified and segregated by religion. Whites lived in upscale neighborhoods like Windsor Farms, which had covenants barring home sales to Jews well into the 1960s. White private clubs, including the Country Club of Virginia, remained strictly off-limits to Jews.

As a practical matter, the segregation was hardly a pressing issue in the lives of ordinary Jews living and working in Richmond. In addition to their own residential enclaves, affluent Jewish residents had their own elite club—Oak Hill, their own private schools, their own sports teams and high school and college fraternities. Their children attended Mary Munford Elementary, Albert Hill Middle School, and Thomas Jefferson High, virtual training camps for high achievers. They had the JCC for sports teams. Oddly enough, the YMCA was open to all.

Joe Rothenberg was successful, but the upper crust Jewish social circles were just out of reach financially. His family frequented the JCC on Monument Avenue or bought a membership in the more modest Three Chopt Pool Association.

Jews had been in Richmond's flood-prone Shockoe Bottom district since the mid–nineteenth century. The first wave of immigrants, primarily from Germany and Austria, was typically educated, possessed of some capital and a fierce desire to assimilate. They moved, for the most part, unremarked into the American mainstream. A second migration—a flood of poor, ragged, illiterate peasants fleeing the shtetls of Russia and the ghettoes of Eastern Europe—followed at the turn of the century. Shedding the beards and black frocks of the Orthodox, they became the rag collectors, scrap metal merchants, peddlers, and purveyors of secondhand furniture and small shopkeepers on the path to the American dream. The Rothenbergs were drawn from both these vibrant streams.

Those gene pools merged into a classic tale of success. The Rothenberg children—Douglas, Stanley, Gail, Gilbert, and Edward excelled academically and professionally, except for Edward, a rebel who came of age in the unsettled '60s.

Their success was not unusual for West End. "We had a fifty-year reunion of the block we grew up on," Stan's kid sister, Gail Rothenberg Lewis, remembered. "When I look back at what all these kids accomplished—a doctor, two lawyers, a couple of business owners—I realize that today we're a continuation of the lifestyle all our parents created for us."

That lifestyle was built on traditional lines. Joseph Rothenberg was a typical 1950s father, the head of the family. He was the breadwinner who labored to provide the new shoes and poodle skirts; the baseball gloves, tools, piano lessons, and color televisions; the summer camps and beach vacations; and the bar mitzvahs and college educations.

"My father wanted the best for his kids," Stanley said, "but always within reason."

Mollie ran the household and the day-to-day rearing of their five children. She made the decisions on all those matters.

The family had all the accoutrements of middle-class respectability, including a station wagon and Mollie's sparkling array of new-fangled, time-saving kitchen gadgets.

The family was as physically active as they were mentally, and that gift and history of athleticism would be a touchstone for Stan during his toughest times. Joe Rothenberg played basketball in high school and continued playing in his thirties and forties at the JCC. He refereed games at the downtown YMCA—he maintained a lifelong membership—more for his love of the game than the few bucks he made.

Joe considered it his duty to inculcate his sons into a range of sports, and one of those was learning to swim at the Y. In Stanley's case, with some unforeseen consequences.

"In those days, it was all male and everyone swam in the nude," Stan recalled. "I was only ten-years-old, but even then, I certainly loved being with physically beautiful men."

Afterward, Joe made a point of taking the boys for burgers and fries at the nearby White Tower, making sure to order extra pickles and never failing to add one of the corny lines that seem to be inbred in all Jewish males of a certain age, no matter where they reside: "I'd rather clothe you guys than feed you!"

As a young man, Stan worked with his father, delivering furniture and collecting debts. Facing the dire poverty and economic distress of their customers bit deep into his soul. Their poverty bought his comfortable lifestyle, and the young, sensitive Stan had a hard time reconciling the two.

But sitting in his father's rundown Plymouth station wagon, the lanky, shy youth forced himself to face the reality of his father's family business.

"Our customers would not have had home furnishings if my grandfather and my dad did not extend them credit," he remembered. "At the same time, the quality of goods was so dismal, many customers would end up owing money on furniture that had long ago broken down."

In contrast to his shy, quiet son, Joe Rothenberg was a happy, upbeat man. He made the daily commute to the store at 1712 East Main Street, a street in a maze of rapidly deteriorating homes and businesses, driving blissfully along the familiar route, ignoring traffic signs. At the family store, he haggled agreeably with his customers, kibitzed with the regulars, the remaining *meshuggeners* and *hondlers* who still lived in Shockoe Bottom. He loved to stop in at the historic farmer's market on 17th Street when the state's famed Hanover tomatoes were in season and occasionally at Weiman's Bakery near the A&P, where he'd pick up the house-special triple-layer cake—each layer a different color and flavor, topped with chocolate icing his kids loved.

Gregarious and with a large circle of friends and acquaintances, he was backslapper, a man's man who loved sports and card games at the JCC, but also a mensch people relied on when things went wrong. He'd tell a joke, get halfway through, and forget the punch line to his embarrassment and the delight of his listeners. He was affectionate with his wife and warm with his children, particularly with Gail, whom he favored as his "Sugarplum."

Stan's mother, Mollie Faye (Drazin) Rothenberg was a perfect complement to Joe. Tall, with dark eyes and dark brown hair with natural golden glints, she was Joe's match in intelligence and ambition. They were a team, working together to build that new life for their children.

Mollie was born in Elmira, New York, and raised in a broken home. At the turn of the century, divorce, with or without a rabbinical "get," was not uncommon among impoverished Eastern European Jews, particularly in situations where husbands arrived in America first and often lived separated from their families for years.

After her divorce, Mollie's mother, Sarah, relocated her five children to Washington, DC, Mollie graduated from Walt Whitman High School, took commercial courses, and worked for a time, according to family legend, as a secretary in FDR's White House.

A devoted wife and mother, Mollie was determined that the upheavals of her uncertain and insecure childhood would never afflict her family. This, she decided early on, required iron discipline as much as nurturing;

she wouldn't hesitate to enforce her standards by force of will and occasionally with the assistance of an old fashioned leather strap.

"My mother cared deeply about her children's welfare," Stanley recalled with a touch of sadness. "She never wanted harm to find any of us."

Mollie got up early each morning and busied herself getting her husband off to work, rousting the children, packing lunches and fixing pancakes, oatmeal, or cereal for breakfast, pouring each child tall glasses of creamy milk delivered three times a week by truck from the Richmond and Curles Neck dairies. She was unmistakably a woman of her age, a time when *The Jetsons* rather than *The Simpsons* defined the zeitgeist. Mollie was big on innovative, time-saving gadgets. In the evenings, she whipped up milkshakes in her gleaming Waring blender and sewed clothes on her Sears Kenmore sewing machine.

She tracked the household budget, handled shopping and grocery-buying, oversaw the cleaning lady and the gardener who trimmed the hedges and mowed the lawn, orchestrated the annual family vacation to Virginia Beach. It was she—with Joe's consent—who decided to install air-conditioning on the ground floor of the house, to glass-in the porch, and to convert the lights from incandescent to cheaper fluorescent.

"She was always forward-looking," Stanley remembered. "But unfortunately in her mind, the cost of fluorescent lighting always trumped a warmer glow."

Just as Joe's passion for sports was a touchstone of Stan's later life, so was Mollie's careful management of their finances.

Mollie was the arbiter and enforcer, the avatar of disciplined, no-nonsense, success-oriented parenting. She held inclusive family meetings open to the children, that in Stanley's telling, were as democratic as a Soviet-era election. She brooked no challenge once she made a decision.

In the 1950s, one of Mollie's primary duties was to make sure her children were on a solid path to success. That meant suppressing adolescent rebellion and independence. According to Stan, Mollie had little feel for the warmth and outsized affection associated with Jewish mothers. Even Gail's remembrance, delivered in the course of a long afternoon's interview, was revealing, particularly because she loved her mother completely and unconditionally: "It was easier for her to communicate her feelings in words."

Unlike Gail, Stanley had a catalog of grievances against his mother, in particular her authoritarian streak ("She was cerebral to the point that she'd come across as a know-it-all.") and her unpredictability.

"She kept a paperback volume of Dr. Spock on a side table in the living room and a thick leather strap in the kitchen drawer," he said, remembering, in detail, every spanking she ever administered.

When they were growing up, Douglas and Gilbert were the family superstars. Stan's older brother Doug was a mechanical genius who, as a teenager, converted a room in the family basement into a *Back to the Future* workshop churning out go-karts and other whiz-bang inventions. He graduated from Virginia Tech with a degree in electrical engineering and went on to earn a PhD. His pioneering work on systems and control engineering was internationally recognized. In fact, he wrote a book on the subject: *Alarm Management for Process Control.*

Younger brother Gil graduated from the University of Pennsylvania and earned a law degree at American

University. Gil was a top-ranking government official—
chief of the Appellate Section of the Department of
Justice's Tax Division. As kids, Stan and Gil often butted
heads, sometimes coming to blows. Obviously, his brother's arrest on child porn charges shook the buttoned-down
Gil to his core, but he helped Stan weather the first days of
the arrest and helped him find his first attorney.

■ ■ ■

More sensitive and less resilient than either Doug or Gil,
Stan had a rockier path forward. Gangly, insecure, self-con-
scious, lonely, and frustrated, he was teen angst and anxiety
personified. Stanley struggled with his burgeoning sexuality. Between his experiences swimming naked at the YMCA
and the confusing and compelling times in the locker
rooms at the JCC, it was increasingly clear to him that he
was physically attracted to men.

But that wasn't possible in the 1950s in Richmond, not
if he were to fulfill the dreams his parents had for him.
Instead of being a member of the prosperous middle class,
he was a sinner and an outcast. He came of age at a time
and place where homosexuality was at best designated a
strain of mental illness. Euphemistically and derisively, he
was defined by "the love that dare not speak its name."

In truth, the adolescent Stanley didn't know exactly
what he was, but given the world he inhabited, he suspected it was awful. Homosexuals were "queers" who
lurked in public toilets and cruised Byrd Park after dark.

No one saw Stan's pain. It was right there, if anyone
had bothered to truly look at him. If anyone had truly
cared about the frightened, confused teenager. Outwardly,
the signs of his inner turmoil were all there: picking at

his cuticles, twisting his hair, making lists, and scribbling voluminous notes to himself, trying desperately to impose structure and order on his anxious mind just as his mother imposed order on their family.

Along with his father's love of sports and his mother's financial acumen, Stan carried all those obsessive anxiety behaviors into adulthood where they metastasized into full-blown, self-destructive compulsions.

At Thomas Jefferson High, Stan overcompensated, driving himself academically, eager to earn a measure of praise from a perfectionist mother. In his memory, this rarely happened.

"One evening I was sitting at my bedroom desk studying my history book and idly playing with my hair," he recalled. "My mother popped her head in to tell me something. Whatever it was, she ended by saying, 'Only girls play with their hair!'" Such long-ago hurt was a constant in Stan's memories, another *cri de coeur.*

But the world was worried about more than just an anguished gay teenager in a large family living in a conservative Southern city. The Cold War simmered and the threat of mutual assured destruction sent students scrambling under their desks during air raid drills.

The first physical manifestations of Stan's anxiety surfaced in connection with his religion. As expected, Stan put in four years of Hebrew School at Richmond's Conservative Temple, Beth-El, memorized his Torah portion, and made his Bar Mitzvah on May 18, 1957.

He also came late to puberty. Later, he would swear his falsetto chanting of the *haftarah* would rival Michael Jackson. (He pleaded with his parents to purchase a reel-to-reel tape recorder to capture this ethereal sound before his voice changed, a request vetoed because of cost.)

Stan dutifully attended weekly services and Sunday school all through high school. "I was never a religious person," he recalled. "My parents literally forced me and this caused friction between us." In addition to the anxiety he was already suffering over his sexuality, being forced to attend services pushed him over the edge.

Stan started "blocking." It happened at Temple one day. Rabbi Jacob Milgrom, an esteemed biblical scholar, was droning on in a flat and lifeless monotone. Next to Stan, Joe started dozing as soon as Milgrom got underway, jolting awake whenever Mollie dug an elbow into his side. Under Mollie's watchful eyes, Stan had little choice but to try to appear like he was listening to the sermon.

Suddenly, the rabbi's words quit making sense. Stan could hear the individual words but they were just sounds skimming across the surface of his mind. They made no sense. No matter how hard he concentrated, he couldn't understand what the rabbi was saying. (Many years later, a psychologist who administered an advanced battery of tests would come up with more precise term for this malfunction.)

Over the next years, the blocking ate up more aspects of his life. Spoken exchanges among more than two persons flew by him. A TV series, a novel, or a movie plot shattered into confused shards of disconnected information. Stan was never among the millions of Americans who followed each twist and turn of *Star Trek* or *Friends*. He simply couldn't follow what was going on.

The disconnect was far-reaching and carried far greater consequences than what was often simplified into an attention deficit disorder. Try as he might, forging a clear connection between the conceptual and the empirical, fantasy and fact, cause and effect, and processing that information in order make logical extrapolations—the very elements of understanding—eluded him.

True to the management skills he'd picked up from his mother, Stan tried to conceal the deficits his blocking caused. He made lists, took notes, and committed enormous numbers of facts to memory and recited them back on demand, a process that left him frustrated and anxious because his acquired knowledge leaked away like water in a sieve.

While Stan was channeling his mother's organizational skills to fight the blocking, he was also trying to learn his gregarious father's skills. Internally wracked by insecurity and ineffable loneliness, he compensated, developing an outsized passion for baseball that would stay with him all the way into adulthood. He taught himself to dance; he practiced telling jokes with his best buddy Allen Sinsheimer; he joined Aleph Zadik Aleph, (AZA, a high school fraternity for Jewish boys not cool enough to make the cut at the more desirable Upsilon Lambda Phi). He suffered through his mom's mandated piano lessons.

Despite it all, Stan remained an outsider: "It seemed to me that other Jews discriminated against me, as much as or more so than non-Jews," he remembered.

He was hardly alone in failing to fit in. Gay men of a certain age all endured this overwhelming sense of otherness. Society literally denied and derided the very rhythms of their bodies, the yearnings of their hearts, and their very notion of self. Of course this cloud of shame and confusion loomed over the young Stanley Rothenberg. On another level, he was just a boy who wanted to be a part of things and didn't know how—an adolescent eager to experience his first crush, to pass a flirty note in class, to walk a sweetheart home from school, to spend hours talking on the phone—unfulfilled yearnings that would curdle and haunt him for the rest of his life.

Despite Stan's awkwardness and blocking—or perhaps because it forced him to draw on his parents' skills—he earned good enough grades at Thomas Jefferson High to win admission to Virginia's well-regarded College of William & Mary. This would prove a pyrrhic victory as the stressors in his life only intensified behind the pleasant and leafy facade of colonial Williamsburg.

Seven

FALL WAS LATE coming that year. As colleges started their fall terms, the leaves had not yet started to turn. Mornings were warm and long, with only a hint of crispness in the evening to hint at the changing seasons.

More than the seasons were changing. Stan was leaving home to start his first year of college.

As with so many things in his life, it was a compromise. The college was small enough that Stan was convinced he'd be more than just a number. At the same time, he felt a longing for the anonymity a larger campus would provide. But with his brother already in college and William & Mary just an hour down the road, he'd convinced himself it was the logical choice.

Joe Rothenberg was not a rich man, so travel and cost were obvious considerations in reaching a decision. William & Mary was a public institution, so tuition, given the fact that his parents were already shouldering the cost of his brother Doug's education at Virginia Tech, was a less onerous burden than an out-of-state college.

■ ■ ■

Stan woke early on move-in day. He'd barely slept at all, anxiety and excitement roiling through his brain and guts, insanely eager to leave yet terrified that his blocking would damn him to failure.

He checked in early, relying on the map of the campus he'd memorized so that he wouldn't get lost or look so new. The morning passed in a flurry of class schedules, book buying, and locating places to eat. He kept a folded map tucked into the pocket of his khaki pants just in case his memory failed him. By midafternoon, the edges were grimy from being rubbed, but he'd managed to navigate most of his schedule without referring to it.

Eventually, he made his way to Yates Hall, the newest dorm on the campus. He trotted up the stairs, enjoying the heady feeling of freedom and adulthood.

On the third floor, he walked down the hall to room 334, then paused outside the door and collected his thoughts. Although he'd shared a room with his brother Doug, this would be his first nonfamily roommate, another new experience. What would it be like to share a room with a stranger? He shuddered a bit but then decided to expect the best.

He knocked once—should he knock? After all, it was his own room!—then used his key to let himself in.

His new roommate had evidently been there and gone out again. A stack of books covered one desk and a few suitcases littered the bed. He felt a moment of relief that he hadn't had to decide which bed was his, coupled with a slight annoyance that he'd had no choice.

Just then, the door opened—no knock!—and a stranger charged in, grinning, energy and cheerfulness radiating out from him. The stranger was shorter than Stan—most people were—and had dark eyes, dark curly hair, and the solid build of a wrestler.

"Hi, roomie!' the stranger said, holding out his hand. "I'm Bob."

Stan's roommate was Robert "Bob" Zentz, an affable, outgoing young man from Norfolk, Virginia. Over that first semester, two Jewish kids (an anomaly at W&M) became friendly despite some looming differences. For one thing, Zentz was straight. Secondly, in the spirt of the era, Zentz loved folk music. (In 1962, Peter, Paul and Mary and Peter Seeger were the big names on many campuses, not just for their music, but also for their social activism.) Zentz was a guitar and banjo aficionado who organized hootenannies and sing-alongs, not exactly someone with whom the straight-laced Stan (he favored jitterbugging and big bands) could feel totally at ease around.

■ ■ ■

After Harvard, William & Mary is the second-oldest college in the United States. Founded in 1693, it numbers Presidents Thomas Jefferson, James Monroe, and John Tyler number among its alumni. More recent grads include investment banker Kenneth Langone, who helped fund Home Depot, former Secretary of Defense Robert Gates, actress Glenn Close, and comedian Jon Stewart.

But Stan wasn't thinking about the illustrious alumni. He wasn't even thinking about classes, majors, and careers.

The main thing on his mind was the intriguing opportunity to freely explore his sexuality.

"I had this intense buildup of unexpressed testosterone. But I didn't know where to meet other gays or even how to meet them," he recalled. "I felt just like every other gay boy of seventeen—naïve, awkward, frustrated, and completely terrified.

"How could I come out? Where? With whom? I'd been raised in a bubble. My parents controlled what I did and where I went.

"It would have been okay if I were straight, but I wasn't. I was different, very secretly different. Telling my mom that I had strong feelings for guys would have opened a can of worms I never would have been able to deal with."

Despite his preoccupation with sex, Stan had chosen a challenging pre-med track that included biology, chemistry, math, and English literature.

"That first semester, academics took all my time," he recalled. "I had little interest in extracurricular activities."

But his schedule wasn't the real reason he avoided digging into campus life. The truth was that he was afraid of rejection and ostracism. Despite his best efforts, he'd never managed to fit in during high school, but at least he'd been at a primarily Jewish high school. But now even that common culture had been ripped away from him.

No one with a name like Rothenberg was on any list of "good-gets" among the WASPs on fraternity row. And sure enough, Pi Lambda Phi, the predominately Jewish fraternity at W&M, ignored him as well. Zentz was outraged by the snub and refused his bid from Pi Lambda Phi in solidarity with Stan.

"It was probably for the best," Stan said. "I'd have been living a lie on fraternity row."

Stan's first semester at William & Mary passed uneventfully. Stan studied hard and finished the semesters with a 3.0 GPA. As he fell into a routine, his anxiety lessoned. He and Bob became good friends.

But despite his most ardent fantasies, Stan finished his first semester as a virgin.

Second semester, as the bleak Tidewater winter waned and spring arrived, Stan's thoughts turned to baseball. As a kid, he loved to play the outfield. He'd been rangy and talented at the position that afforded him a chance to think and daydream.

But Stan didn't dare try out for the William & Mary team. "Anxiety prevented me," he later said. "I couldn't perform in front of crowds. I knew I'd choke." Instead, he volunteered to be the team equipment manager, an offer the coach happily accepted.

Soon enough, Stan was chasing foul balls hit into the bushes that rimmed the first base line, even hitting fungoes to the outfielders. "I loved every minute of it," he said.

Baseball at William & Mary was not the high-profile sport with a big budget and the sort of rabid fan base that defines so many collegiate athletics programs today. The team shared a makeshift locker room with a kinesiology class, which meant that occasionally, a cadaver greeted the astonished players as they suited up.

Just as he had at the YMCA pool, Stan had other more lively interests. "My favorite part was being in the locker room with twenty-odd handsome, hunky men," he said. "They were quite sexy in their tight-fitting uniforms but even more so with them off."

He settled for fantasies mostly, save for one fumbling encounter with a horny and sexually confused player he encountered on a road trip to South Carolina.

"This hunky outfielder actually hopped in my bed when the other players weren't around," Stan said. "He started to hunch me while we were fully clothed. I was so startled I rejected the offer."

The joy and calm he drew from the baseball squad helped him keep his grades up, his academics on track, and his insecurities at bay. He stayed on as equipment manager for four years, occasionally branching out into sports writing, submitting playful stories to the school paper about The Tribe, as the team was known.

But the sensitive, anxious Stan still lurked just under the surface of the dependable equipment manager. On November 22, 1963, he was in the chemistry lab, trying to puzzle out his notes and figure out how to approach analyzing the contents of the vial in front of him. There were procedures, elements you had to test for first, safety precautions, myriad details that kept flitting through his mind, refusing to assemble themselves into any sort of order.

Just when he thought he was making some progress, the door to the lab opened. His chemistry professor, not just the lab assistant or graduate student, came in. Without any preparatory statement, he said, "President Kennedy was shot this afternoon in Dallas."

"My professor was so matter-of-fact when he made the announcement, it took a few seconds to register in my head," Stan said. "I put away my test tubes and went back to my dorm room.

Stan was immediately and utterly devastated.

Those were the Camelot years. JFK and Jackie had seemed to him the avatars of a kinder, gentler, and certainly sexier America. In some parts of the South and West, the reaction to the president's murder was at best dispassionate, and in some places, celebratory.

"That night I lay in my bunk, tears rolling down my cheeks. I was apolitical and wanted no part of any civil unrest, but the assassination was personal to me. I played Peter, Paul and Mary's "Blowin' in the Wind" and "Stewball" over and over. Until then, my life had been, relatively speaking, peaceful. No world war, no economic depressions, no assassinations. Optimism was definitely in the air. People felt good about life. It all ended abruptly and without warning."

■ ■ ■

The next year, in the fall of '64, Stan switched his major to psychology. Pre-med had lost whatever appeal it had for him in a confused haze of chemistry and calculus courses.

He was still a virgin.

■ ■ ■

Late one winter afternoon, Stan was sitting in a lecture hall, jotting furious notes on the ethics of practice, trying to concentrate as the professor droned on. In general, he liked the psychology courses much more than the science-heavy pre-med track. He kept thinking that there might be some mystic moment in a course where he'd suddenly get an answer that made sense of his life, that would show him a way to deal with his pervasive otherness. He particularly liked the clinical courses that focused on aberrant behavior, the ones that delved deep into the outliers of human behavior. It sent a kind of a thrill through him to read about them.

But ethics and principles of practice were the worst. Dull professors droned on about theoretical situations that were completely useless and contrived, Nevertheless, they were courses he had to pass, so he forced himself to take notes.

"All of a sudden, I stopped being able to comprehend the lecture," he said. "My head just ceased working. I could hear each word fine. However, the more I tried to comprehend the meaning of the words, the more I suffered a mental block."

His blocking had come roaring back. "Listening is not a conscious behavior," he said. "It is subconscious, automatic, like breathing. Mentally, I couldn't breathe! An intense anxiety swept through my body. I was so terrified I thought I might be dying. I staggered back to my dorm room."

The terrifying episode—whatever it was—continued for hours. Stan was forced to endure it alone and without any kind of support. Later, when the panic began to recede, he began to make the first tentative connections between what befell him in the lecture hall and his inability to follow Rabbi Milgrom's sermons at Beth-El, or the movie plots and group conversations, and so many other situations.

Many years later, he would come to understand these early episodes as symptoms of a debilitating illness that muddled his comprehension and decision-making ability for much of his life, and no doubt, set the stage for the series of disastrous choices that would ultimately undo him.

Stan kept his "breakdown" hidden, yet another secret to keep from unforgiving and judgmental eyes. Being deemed "mentally ill" would not play with his psych professors, and he had a career and a future livelihood to keep in mind.

"I stopped having eye contact because I feared people would figure out I was blocking them, and they would embarrass and humiliate me," he remembered. "I didn't block when I read my textbooks, so I read and reread every word, underlining key phrases and highlighting constantly. I borrowed other peoples' notes and wrote all of it down. I did everything I could think of to ease my anxiety, hoping it would go away."

Of course, it didn't go away. It never would. And his fear became obsessive. On holiday break in Richmond, Stanley made a secret appointment with George and Lois Kriegman, a married couple remembered locally as the first Freudian practitioners south of the Mason-Dixon Line.

"It was a disaster. Just the battery of tests Lois Kriegman administered triggered rounds of debilitating anxiety. I was a mess," he recalled. "I thought I'd done poorly."

Whatever the results, he pleaded with Kriegman, "not to tell my parents." He never followed up.

"Blocking and my inability to stop obsessing over it became an integral part of my psyche," Stan said.

Stan graduated from William & Mary in June 1966, as uncertain about the road forward as when he first arrived in Williamsburg. His great love in college was not the sensitive, caring, and erotic encounter with a likeminded young man he fantasized over, but the baseball squad. "Had I not had the team to lean on," he said, "I doubt I ever could have graduated."

He was still a virgin.

■ ■ ■

A generation later, an ambitious young Indian American named Rinku Talwar earned her law degree at William & Mary's Marshall-Wythe School. Talwar walked the same paths, studied in the same libraries, greeted the same fragrant springs as Stan. In 2008, Talwar, an Assistant US Attorney for the Southern District of Florida, would bring the full weight of the law down on Stanley Rothenberg's head.

Eight

STAN'S ELEGANT LIFE filled with simple and comforting routines had dissolved into an unsolved Rubik's Cube. Denied bail, he'd been in jail for three months. While he watched in horror, his personal life disintegrated. His mortgage on his beachside condo went unpaid, financial instability loomed, his friends and relationships were falling apart. He missed critical medical appointments and medication refills that kept him able to cope with life. He lived in limbo, aching for the stable and mundane life he once had, dreading what hell the future might hold.

Stan faced two federal felony counts, and although he didn't know it then, each held the possibility of enhancement. Stan kept running numbers in his head, trying to come up with what would be a "fair punishment" if he were found guilty.

Like a lot of defendants, Stan still believed that his attorney might be able to make it all go away, make everything right. After all, hadn't Metz gotten him a fast transfer from the hellhole in Port St. Lucie to the more amenable Palm Beach County Jail? And Metz had persuaded someone in the medical chain of command to reinstate—though at a lower dosage—Stan's antianxiety medication. An attorney who could get all that done, in contrast to the first guy, had to have a lot on the ball. It would all be resolved, he kept telling himself. Metz would make them see the truth, and then they'd have to let him go.

Metz, however, knew that he wasn't a magician. The prosecution had some serious evidence and by then it was clear that the charges wouldn't simply go away on their own.

During a blunt and very unsettling session with Stan, Metz convinced Stan to plead innocent and go to trial. The fact that the government wins 95 percent of all the criminal prosecutions it took to trial was, for the moment, forgotten. Stan believed that if he could get in front of a jury of his peers and just explain what happened, it would all be dismissed.

Stan waited for a trial date, fighting to keep himself together as the bureaucratic machinery ground him up, trying his best not to listen to his own doubts and insecurities.

The jailhouse lawyers didn't make it any easier. Everybody who had ever read a case book had an opinion on how Stan's case ought to be handled, and they were all very convincing in their analysis.

Like every desperate prisoner awaiting trial since time immemorial, Stan went over the alleged crime again and again, looking at it from every conceivable angle. Detective Spector had twisted and manipulated the evidence from their brief email and phone interaction, turning it into some sinister plot. All Stan had done was go to a parking lot to meet a guy who talked dirty. It was nothing more than a variation of gay cruising, and Stan had known from the second he saw Spector that the self-proclaimed incestuous father wasn't selling anything Stan wanted to buy.

The prosecution was cherry-picking the facts, particularly regarding the second felony. They'd picked out a handful of the most egregious of the printed chats seized from Stan's condo by Fort Lauderdale Detective John Jensen, and tried to turn him into a monster who encouraged fathers to violate their young sons and brothers to rape prepubescent siblings.

It was fantasy role-playing. Why couldn't they see that? There were hundreds of chats in those boxes—hundreds—and only a few were sordid enough to make the prosecution's case. The rest of them were simple, friendly interactions, not fantasy role-playing. The vast majority were just online friendships and inquiries about occupations, educational, interests, and so on. Most of them—like all the legal porn seized from his condo—were homosexual.

"I was looking for cyber friends to ease my loneliness," Stan explained. "I had to try something. So why not assume the role of the perv and act out?"

Stan was certain that if he just explained it to everyone, they'd understand. He looked forward to mounting a vigorous defense. In a courtroom, before a jury of his peers, his powerhouse attorneys, Metz and his partner, Richard Lubin, were going to shred the prosecution's case, hacking apart the flimsy evidence and lies and distortions until unvarnished truth was inescapable. Stan was certain of it.

The jail house lawyers agreed with him. Entrapment, they'd told him, was a solid defense.

■ ■ ■

Stan tried to stay positive. Each assurance from a fellow inmate that he had a rock-solid defense kept him going, kept hope alive. There would be a time when he looked back on all of it and could laugh. Maybe.

But the doubts kept creeping in. Why didn't Metz or Lubin ever ask what the hell Stan was doing in the FamLuv chat room in the first place?

Why didn't they ask about the boxes of chat transcripts? They wanted evidence? There was evidence. It proved what he'd been saying all along—that he was gay and completely uninterested in females or children.

He'd kept the chat transcripts like a teenager keeps the scribbled phone numbers of near-strangers and for the same reasons. To prove that other men found him desirable and that he had friends to chase off the loneliness. On the off chance that maybe he'd actually hook up with one of them someday. And so he could keep his stories straight.

But what he really wanted most of all was: "I was hoping to get my sex organ active again."

In August 2008, Metz showed up at the Palm Beach County jail for a client visit. To Stan's dismay, Metz didn't talk about the preparations for trials, didn't have a list of experts he wanted to call, and didn't even go over the case with Stan so that they could build a stout defense based on Stan's mindset and motives. To Stan's utter shock, Metz counseled him to change his innocent plea to guilty. Given the facts, he assured his rattled client, the best hope was to negotiate a generous plea bargain with the prosecutors.

Simply put, a plea bargain is an arrangement in which a defendant agrees to plead guilty to a particular charge (or charges) in return for concessions from the government. Both parties avoid the time and expense of a lengthy trial, and the defendant avoids the very real risk (more than 90 percent) of being convicted on all counts and finding himself subject to the trial judge's (egged on by a pissed-off prosecution) draconian vengeance.

Ideally, Stan would plead guilty to two Title 18 felonies; in return, the judge would hand down a lenient sentence.

Of course, it wouldn't be that simple. A plea arrangement was a recommendation to the court, not a binding agreement. But with a negotiated plea in hand, a defendant was likely to avoid any untoward surprises. Most judges accept such deals as a matter of course, unless they are illegal or found to be completely inconsistent with the facts of the case.

Metz's advice seemed spot-on. An overwhelming percentage of all federal criminal cases end in plea arrangements. Of the tiny minority who go to trial, nine out of ten defendants are convicted and subject to the full weight of the law.

In 2012, for example, the average sentence for drug offenders convicted after a trial was three times higher (approximately sixteen years) than for defendants who plea-bargained themselves out of harm's way (five years and four months). For sex offenders, particularly those accused of crimes against children, sentences could be astronomical. Despite the lurid legal dramas covered on TV—O.J. Simpson, Timothy McVeigh, John Gotti, and Scott Peterson were three prominent examples—courtroom trials were rare, and justice (or injustice) was typically meted out behind closed doors.

To move forward with a deal, Stan would have to submit a formal Change of Plea to Magistrate Judge Frank

Lynch Jr. who had been handling the preliminary rounds of the case. The presiding judge, US District Court Judge Donald. L. Graham, would have to sign off on any deals.

Metz told Stan that he was already in negotiations with the prosecutor, Assistant US Attorney Rinku Talwar. Unofficially, Metz said, she was offering twenty years in exchange for a guilty plea.

"I told Metz to forget it," Stan said. "It took me twenty-two seconds to come up with that answer!"

Metz went back to Talwar to approach her boss, US Attorney R. Alexander Acosta, with a proposal for a fifteen-year sentence.

"I told Metz to forget that, too!" Stan fumed. "Fifteen years to a sixty-four-year-old man who's never, ever touched a minor in his life? Hell no!"

Stan insisted that when he turned down Talwar's second offer, Metz responded, "I would, too."

Stan found it hard to follow all the details of the negotiations with the AUSA and the ever-changing offers. He'd been incarcerated for months, was on his second set of lawyers, and was still suffering the trauma of benzodiazepine withdrawal.

"When I hired Metz, I did have the impression he could wheel and deal," Stan said later. "And that I'd benefit from all his connections. I honestly believed I could depend on Judge Graham to realize the truth about my case and about me."

Reluctantly, he agreed to plead guilty

It was likely Stan didn't grasp the implications of that decision. Maybe he suspected he was doomed—the case against him seemed absolutely airtight. Perhaps his judgment was still impaired or Metz's analysis was cloudy. It was also possible he was clinging to some long-ago, far-away fairy tale belief that everything would turn out for the best.

By rejecting Rinku Talwar's plea bargain offer and pleading guilty, Stan surrendered his right to a jury trial and with it any hope for exoneration. Instead, he would stand naked before Judge Graham with zero assurances. In legal terminology, this was called an open plea—a defendant throwing himself on the mercy of the court.

Among trial lawyers, an open pleading was akin to a Volkswagen Beetle playing chicken with a Mack truck. The defendant stands mute while the defense and the prosecution hammer away at each other, his fate buttressed or eviscerated by law enforcement agents, medical doctors, psychologists, and various expert witnesses who cite complicated research, precedents, and depositions. Judges labor with onerous caseloads and constant demands. Inevitably, humanity, with all its bias and foibles, leaks into every case and every judgment.

Stan's open plea was also considered disrespectful of the prosecution. In effect, he was telling the court that US Attorney Acosta and Assistant US Attorney Talwar were biased and totally overstating the evidence against him.

Stan was convinced that the judge would see through the web of lies.

But not that's how the rest of the world saw it. They saw a man who was admitting he was guilty of sex crimes involving children. They saw that man asking Judge Graham, a conservative George H. W. Bush appointee, to believe that that man was deserving of a lesser sentence.

Stan rolled the dice.

On August 25, after finding that Stan had "freely and voluntarily" entered a guilty plea, Magistrate Lynch recommended to the District Court that Stan's Change of

Plea be accepted. And further, that "the Defendant be adjudicated guilty of the offenses to which he had entered his plea of guilty…that a sentencing hearing be conducted for final disposition of the matter."

"Final disposition of the matter" had a disquieting ring to Stan's ears.

The US Probation Office got to work on the usual Presentence Report. After federal defendants are convicted, probation officers prepare these reports to assist judges in assessing punishment. The report covers a convict's history, family, employment, ability to repay costs of the offense, and how victims were impacted. A report also includes a calculation of possible sentences under federal Guidelines. District court judges rely heavily on these reports. On the other side of the bar, the prosecution and defense ready themselves to challenge or buttress the probation office findings.

To his dismay, Stanley Rothenberg never got to say his piece before Judge Graham. He never got to shout out in court what had been in his mind since May: "For Christ sake, I'm gay! I'm repulsed by females! I don't even like children!"

He had ten weeks to ready himself. On Monday, November 3, at 11 a.m., he would be sentenced by Judge Graham at the US District Courthouse in Fort Pierce.

Nine

IN JUNE, STANLEY Rothenberg graduated from William & Mary with a BS degree in psychology. Reluctantly, he returned to live with his parents in Richmond. Like millions of other liberal arts grads, he saw no clear path ahead, only the vague sense that college had been a terrible disappointment. He was still a virgin and had not fully come to terms with his sexuality. He was still struggling with blocking issues.

Like many politically conservative Southerners, Stan was uneasy with raucous 1960s counterculture and his place in it. Flower power and free love (if only!) sounded fine. The Who, Jefferson Airplane, and Jim Morrison-style anthems to youthful revolution ("They got the guns, but we got the numbers!") were anathema to him. Around him, tens of thousands of young men were being drafted into the military—380,000 in 1966 alone—fodder for the escalating disaster in Vietnam.

Psychology was one of the no-pressure college majors

that offered an intriguing, cool, and undemanding passage through school while one figured out what to do in real life. It was definitely not, as Stan put it, "a hot ticket to corporate America." Still, he enjoyed his psych courses, no surprise given his inner-direction and escalating psychic challenges, and would have pursued a graduate degree if not for his debilitating blocking problems.

"I was very fearful blocking would prevent me from doing a good job in anything I pursued," he said. "Most people greet their first job search after graduation with excitement and anticipation. I was petrified by the thought of what awaited me down the road."

During his final semester at W&M, Stan spotted a notice on a campus billboard and set up an interview with recruiters from the US Public Health Service (PHS), a nonmilitary uniformed service familiar to laymen as the government agency that administers the Centers for Disease Control and Prevention (CDC). Tested, he ranked more qualified than the average applicant ("Middle of the spectrum," he said). Weeks later, to his surprise, he got a job offer, an entry-level epidemiology position tracking outbreaks of venereal disease. His starting salary was $6,036 a year. Given a choice of three locations, he settled on a public health clinic in Jacksonville (Duval County), Florida. He figured it was warm, had about the same population as his hometown, and fielded an AAA baseball team—the Jacksonville Suns—that competed against his beloved Richmond Virginians. And yes, there was a tingle of adventure—pulling up stakes, hitting the road, leaving the humdrum and mundane behind.

He was not exactly Peter Fonda in *Easy Rider*. Hitting the road meant piling his khakis and madras shirts and topsiders into a white '64 Rambler American and waving good-bye to friends and family. To his surprise, his parting with a teary-eyed Mollie Rothenberg was unexpectedly poignant.

Heading straight south, he drove down I-95 for 600 miles, shunted aside every hundred miles by construction and other delays into the rural byways, old-fashioned gas pumps, "meat-and-three" cafes, and occasional Ku Klux Klan billboards dotting the Carolinas and Georgia. He crossed the fertile marshlands of coastal Georgia and passed historic Savannah, Brunswick, and St. Mary's before crossing into the piney woods and silt-clogged estuaries of northern Florida. It was a world of shrimp boats and paper mills, far-removed from the faded glamour of Miami Beach where the magic of Sinatra, Steve Lawrence, and Eydie Gorme and the spectacle of the Fontainebleau and Eden Roc still glimmer along Collins Avenue.

Stanley stayed with a friend of his mother's for a week. He found a tiny efficiency (200 square feet) apartment in one of the egregious, cobbled-together developments—this one at 7713 India Avenue, #160—cut from the sandy scrublands. Stan was frugal, a trait that characterized him throughout his life no matter his financial situation. He arrived at his peach-colored, one-story, flat-roof residence and unloaded the silverware and glasses and few utensils his mother packed for him.

A huffing air conditioner blocked one of his few windows. Furnishings included a chest built into a wall, a ratty, foam-filled sofa that doubled as a bed, and bric-a-brac scavenged from the Salvation Army store. This was Florida, so no doubt there was a scuzzy pool, a couple of sun-cracked tennis courts, and a banged-up soft drink machine among the development's amenities. He did spot a few intriguing-looking men by the pool. All for ninety bucks a month.

It's impossible to overestimate the effect that moving to Florida had on Stan. For a young man raised in Virginia, already facing crippling anxiety and the pressures a young gay man experiences, it was an act of courage, this breaking free of everything he'd lived with before and traveling alone to an environment that he hoped would allow him to be himself.

For Stan, it was freedom. Away from the stifling environment of Virginia, college, and family, he was free. The few boxes of silverware, glasses, and utensils his mother had packed for him weren't enough to anchor him to his prior life. His life was now his own.

And if this were possible, what else might be? Anything. Absolutely anything.

Specifically, Ron M. was possible.

Stan had met the hunky young basketball player while working as a camp counselor one summer in New Hampshire, and Stan had never forgotten him. He'd fallen in love with Ron M. instantly and spent the entire summer dreaming about the tall, attractive, gentle man.

"At camp, I was in love with Ron even though the concept was never discussed," Stan recalled. "We'd exchange seductive glances but nothing ever came of it. I knew in my mind if he'd come to Jacksonville, it all would come together."

But would Ron feel the same way? How could Stan convince Ron to come to Florida?

In trying to balance the heady freedom and empowerment he felt with an underlying sense of unworthiness inculcated by society and his family, Stan began a pattern that would later land him in federal prison. Reconciling the disparate elements gave rise to a fantasy that took on a life of its own, supplanting reality and hyper stimulating him.

What would make Ron want to come to Florida? Just the

chance to see Stan again? No, he couldn't risk that. It had to be an irresistible offer.

Basketball. That would do it. Ron could get a basketball scholarship to Jacksonville University. Ron would move to Florida, and he and Stan could have the searing sexual experiences Stan had been dreaming about for years.

So Stan wrote Ron a letter suggesting Jacksonville University was a "great school to apply to for a basketball scholarship!" (The school was unknown among basketball aficionados.) Then Stan drove out to the campus and barged in on the basketball coach where he sang Ron's praises.

"Have him come by when he gets here," the coach said, shrugging, clearly underwhelmed by Stan.

Stan took that as a win. Now all he had to do was get Ron to Florida to meet the coach and it would all work out. He could see all the details, and they became more vivid every day. The elaborate and overheated sex fantasies and scenarios grew even more real and were profoundly gratifying, setting the pattern that would one day lead to the AOL FamilyLuv chatroom.

But fate intervened. A week before Ron was scheduled to arrive in Jacksonville for his "basketball tryout," Stan's boss sent him to Pensacola, 400 miles away on the Gulf of Mexico. His assignment: participate in an immunization survey in rural Escambia County, literally the westernmost part of the state.

"It shatters my plans to help Ron get a scholarship and our highly anticipated soiree," Stan remembered.

He remained a virgin.

Ten

1967
Jacksonville, Florida

STAN STARED ACROSS the desk at the husky man before him, then glanced down at the folder in front of him to remind himself of the man's name. He'd looked at it just thirty seconds earlier, just before he'd stepped out into the waiting room to call him in, but the name had already evaporated from his mind. Stan wasn't sure whether it was from his blocking syndrome or just a normal occurrence when dealing with a flood of patients every day. It seemed as though for every patient he saw and sent on, two more appeared.

And every single one of them was having more sex than Stan. The endless details and variations both excited and bored him. Submerged in a culture focused daily on the aftermath of casual sex, he was increasingly frustrated by his own virginity.

But it had a couple of advantages. First, the patients' actual experiences provided new fuel for his own rich fantasy life. Second, Stan felt increasingly confident about his own ability to perform well when it eventually happened.

As a newly minted caseworker, Stan followed patients who showed up at the clinic complaining of penile discharges, rashes, discomfort, and other more painful symptoms. More often than not, these turned out to be syphilis and gonorrhea (the clap) infections. Both were treatable but virulently communicable, so it was standard epidemiological practice to track down sexual contacts in the hope of limiting a broader outbreak.

Among the flood passing through the Jacksonville clinic were sailors from the nearby naval air station, an overlapping assortment of prostitutes and IV drug users, and seemingly inordinate numbers of well-educated, white homosexual men.

In 1966, most sexually transmitted diseases (STDs) were successfully treated with antibiotics. Because they were easily cured, patients felt little pressure to change behaviors. Other sexually transmitted viral diseases like genital herpes and hepatitis B had not yet reached epidemic proportions but were on the rise. A decade or more later, in the early 1980s, the great blood-borne plague—HIV and AIDS—spread by hyper-promiscuity, would ravage these populations.

At 9:30 p.m., when the clinic shut down, Stan hopped into his Rambler and headed into the field. His case list often led him to Jacksonville gay bars, cabarets, and other haunts where he hoped to track down particular individuals—often male prostitutes—suspected of wildly spreading STDs.

It wasn't easy. Many of the contacts on his list were anonymous, quickies performed in bathroom stalls, parks, and in the front seats of cars.

In his job, Stan couldn't be further removed from the straight population and its distaste and unease with homosexuals. Given the morbidity of STDs, gay culture was a much discussed topic at staff meetings. Stan absorbed it eagerly. Nothing was taboo.

"We were instructed to acquaint ourselves with gay terms like cruising, gay clichés, and gay promiscuity," he recalled.

One of the books on his list was John Rechy's classic *City of Night*, a street hustler's account of the 1960s homosexual netherworld. Rechy's character, hypersexual yet incapable of love and affection, was desired for his physical beauty yet despised for selling his body. Ultimately, he found himself alone. The book, which gained international prominence, was a foreshadowing of gay culture in the age of AIDS, but Stan wasn't drawing any life lessons from what he was reading. He was young and immortal. Hell, it excited him.

To Stan, shedding his virginity was comparable to a butterfly emerging from a chrysalis. He was also determined to begin dealing with what he was now convinced were deep-rooted psychological traumas and the source of so much of his pain. His tentative attempt to confront the issues with the Kriegman therapists in Richmond had been a debacle. At the time, he couldn't afford their counseling without appealing to his parents, and that was out of the question. In the South, acknowledging psychological dysfunction, or worse, seeking help from a "sy-col-a-gis" was all but declaring himself another Blanche Dubois and Boo Radley. His job, however, provided health insurance, including mental health coverage.

No more hiding his challenges and his sexual orientation from prying eyes. Or so he thought.

At work, Stan was the new guy, and his diffidence about engaging in the usual office banter and flirtations earned him the reputation—he said—"of a Don Juan who's coy and playing hard-to-get with the girls. Nothing could be further from the truth, but I needed to maintain this false identity until I could get well."

Even with medical insurance, he couldn't pay the "exorbitant fees" charged by private practitioners. To his dismay, the only therapist covered by his insurance was a woman whose office was directly behind the public health clinic.

"I knew that it was very risky," he said, "but I was ill and needed help so I signed up."

"Therapy," he said, "consisted of fifty-minute sessions run by a middle-age lady with a controlling temperament." It was supposed to be group therapy, but the only other member of his group, Stan recalled, "was a man who spoke with an obvious lisp and had probably been bullied his entire life and had zero self-esteem." Not exactly the kindred spirit Stan was looking for.

After four sessions, Stan began pulling back. "I was twenty-two years old and had shared that I was still a virgin," he said. "I was a very frustrated gay man who wanted nothing to do with females and this one in particular. Instead, she acted as though she wanted to prove me straight by casually trying to seduce me! All this was making my blocking issues and coming out much more difficult."

1967
Miami, Florida

As part of his in-service training, Stan attended a number of statewide epidemiological conferences. At one, he met Fred Halper, a venereal disease (VD) investigator based in Dade County, Florida. Fred lived with his wife and young child near the beach in North Miami. With its heavily ethnic, northeastern-influenced, and outspokenly brash culture, Miami Beach was a world removed from Jacksonville, which straddled, psychically and physically, the Georgia border. The two young men, both Jewish, hit it off, exchanged phone numbers, and promised to stay in touch.

Miami was as different from Jacksonville as Jacksonville was from Virginia, and Stan was immediately captivated by the culture. The heady freedom he'd felt in Jacksonville had quickly faded. After one year there, with no friends, no respite from his blocking, and a looming sense of failure despite his best efforts, Stan Rothenberg was ready for a change. He applied for and was granted a transfer to a public health clinic in Dade County.

In 1967, Miami was awakening from decades of somnolence, en route to becoming the cosmopolitan, high-energy international city it is today. On the streets radiating outward from Calle Ocho, the heart of downtown Miami, Spanish was fast displacing English as a lingua franca. The Cuban exile community had taken root, bolstered by a massive influx of well-heeled, stylish Columbians, Venezuelans, and other Latinos who bought and sold estates and luxury condos on Brickell Avenue and flew in and out, trailing wives and mistresses and children on extravagant shopping sprees. A few of them were the gaudy, dangerous drug dealers caricatured in *Miami Vice* and *Scarface*.

Waves of cocaine cowboys, smugglers, and flamboyant drug dealers were on the horizon. South Beach's Art Deco District was showing the first signs of life: artists, designers, the avant garde, and hangers-on slowly displaced Yiddish-speaking Jewish retirees from the Bronx and Brooklyn. Nightlife—discos, private clubs, upscale restaurants—was throbbing to the nonstop beat of salsa and Afro-Cuban rhythms. Newly liberated gays were flocking to the beach, adding another flavor to the cultural stew. Further up Miami Beach, the Fontainebleau Hotel was about to undergo a billion-dollar renovation.

Amidst the tropic heat and sexual energy, Stanley Rothenberg discovered a thriving gay community. He moved into a one-bedroom apartment in Coral Gables in the fall of 1967.

When Joe Rothenberg shipped his son a set of twin beds from the Richmond store, the always-frugal Stan took out an ad for a roommate. Barry W., a University of Miami student, showed up. Barry was also Jewish, but unfortunately, Stan realized, that was all the two men had in common.

Over the next months, Stan fell in love with the cosmopolitan feel of the city, the crowds, the beaches, the pastel houses, the turquoise ocean, and the endless possibilities. He and Fred Halper ("tons of fun"), whom he'd met at the convention, reconnected and began spending lots of time together outside the office. Sometimes, Stan recalled, the two role-played, taking turns impersonating a VD investigator and a swishing gay subject.

"To learn better interview techniques," Stan said, but in reality it was a kind of clumsy, uncertain seduction.

Settled into a routine at the clinic, Stanley began searching for a competent psychotherapist. In a pre-internet world—no search engines, no websites to explore, no online rankings of medical professionals—that meant basically just word of mouth, an internist's recommendation, or when all else failed, the *Yellow Pages.*

He picked Dr. Thomas Doody out of the phone book. Young, soft-spoken, reassuring, and hip, Doody came across as the polar opposite of the strident female therapist he'd seen in Jacksonville. Doody lived on a houseboat in Coconut Grove, a heavily-gay area. His office was on the first floor of a stately home off Brickell Avenue near downtown Miami, the kind of soothing, tasteful place Stan imagined a therapist should inhabit.

Of course, Stan wound himself up and obsessed over the appointment, but once there, he quickly felt his anxiety melting away. Doody listened carefully as Stan described the blocking that had so disrupted his life, the sexual frustration, and his feelings of otherness and isolation. He came away clinging to the first possibility of hope and a prescription for Librium (later switched to Valium) and a calendar marked with twice-a-week appointments.

Euphoria and hope surged through Stan. "My life might be in for a major change for the better!"

Stan had the prescriptions filled that same day. "I took my initial dose, and within half-an-hour I felt like a totally different person," he recalled. "The tingling in my upper thighs (a manifestation of severe anxiety) disappears! For the first time in my life, I actually feel no anxiety whatsoever. I can look people in the eye and not have to turn away. I could concentrate. I literally stopped blocking that day. I've been reborn."

Librium is a benzodiazepine, an antianxiety drug that works by slowing the movement of chemicals in the brain, resulting in a decrease in anxiety, muscle spasms, and other symptoms. In 1967, not much was known about the long-term side effects and potential for addiction.

Stan didn't care.

"With a script for Librium," he recalled, "coming to grips with my sexuality was a piece of cake. Miami and its environs have many gay bars, so it was just a matter of my staying up very late one weekend and hanging out."

Because the Miami VD clinic saw a big incidence of gay anal gonorrhea, he convinced himself he was "trying to track down sexual contacts from my work interviews." In this hothouse environment, sex was as casual as slipping into a bathroom stall. Among other things, Stan discovered that he was a "top" or what epidemiologists defined as "anal-insertive."

One Wednesday night, surveying the raucous gay scene at the Alley Bar in Miami Beach, Stan spotted "Paul," a young, very handsome prostitute who previously visited the VD clinic for treatment of anal gonorrhea. Paul's case history indicated he'd had anonymous sex with dozens of men in the previous month alone. Paul could not name a single one.

An hour later, the two were "having mad, passionate sex at my apartment," he recalled. "At the time, the hottest sex I'd ever experienced and will never forget."

In addition to losing his virginity, Stan learned that he was not so different from Paul or millions of other gay men in those days. Despite all his fantasies, both sexual and romantic, he never learned Paul's last name.

Of course, Stan told his friends about his sexual experience, among them Fred, who was coming to terms with identity issues of his own. "Fred quickly became amenable to investigating the gay experience," Stan recalled. "He'd been told so much by his gay clients that he wanted to try out this unique and freewheeling way of life. The easiest way was for us to have sex with each other. So we do. Fred's coming out party wouldn't have won any Oscar nominations, but the event enriched both of us. We'd laugh about it for decades to come." To this day, Fred Halper remains one of Stan's closest friends.

Nearly fifty years later, looking back on his time in Miami, Stan reflected, "Already, I was very comfortable in my own skin, I'd become the person I have known since childhood that I am."

And so it began. Like innumerable young, liberated gay men, Stan went on to have sex with dozens, perhaps even hundreds of men, mostly anonymous encounters. While the numbers might sound overstated, investigators working for the CDC in the early '80s have evidence to support it. Their epidemiological reports show that some of the earliest diagnosed AIDS patients—young, gay males living in New York City, Los Angeles, Miami, and San Francisco—had engaged in anonymous sex with thousands of partners.

The Swinging Sixties: drugs, sex, and rock & roll, the counterculture, free love, rebellion, Woodstock. Among straight people, the Pill unleashed a similar flood of easy and unencumbered sex that streamed unchecked into the millennium and beyond. Gay culture, long repressed, derided, and forced into the shadows, seethed for its own expression. Sex became its ethos and its essence. Gay men didn't require birth control. They didn't marry. For the

overwhelming majority, mortgages, long-term commitment, children, and tuition were not on the radar. Unlike
HIV and debilitating infections like hepatitis B, STDs
were not life-threatening and, as Stan discovered, were
treated and shrugged off.

Without question, a recklessness evident in a willingness to do anything, try anything, be anything, and
indulge in any fantasy or erotic behavior characterized many of these young men. On one level, it was a
long-overdue slap at straight males who considered
themselves the macho ideal and derided gay men as fags
and sissies. This recklessness was rampant in the bathhouses and orgy rooms, in the gay bars on the Hudson
River in the West Village, on Castro Street in San Francisco, on Key West and Fire Island, in Washington, DC,
Los Angeles, and Miami. Inevitably, it fueled an even
more dramatic explosion of STDs, spikes in drug and
alcohol abuse, and other destructive behaviors. Ultimately, despite cries of denial in the gay community, it led
to the AIDS apocalypse.

In the twenty-first century, the AIDS epidemic and
encroaching age forced changes on a large segment of the
population. As they grew older and less sexually appealing, the hot-blooded promiscuous young men who'd
made Miami what it was mourned the youthful freedom,
excitement, pleasure, and liberation they'd felt. The world
they remembered faded further and further away.

Fortunately, for some, especially those who adored the
fantasy almost as much as the actuality, technology provided solutions. The chat room replaced the bathhouse as
a source of gratification.

Stan, Fred, and Jerry remained close friends over the
next half-century. They survived the AIDS epidemic, only

to face other challenges. Jerry moved to California (he retired as a Merrill-Lynch vice president). He had battled both lung and stomach cancer. Fred, diagnosed with late-stage kidney disease, had been on dialysis for a decade. And Stanley? Like the ancient mariner, he was spared to share his tale of catastrophe and woe.

Eleven

FOUR DECADES LATER, a listless Stanley Rothenberg marked the days until his December 10 sentencing at the district courthouse in Fort Pierce, alternating between utter despair and an occasional flicker of hope.

After talking with his attorney, Michael Metz, Stan reluctantly changed his plea to guilty on both counts.

Count One: *18 USC. § 2422(b). 1 e.* Using a computer in interstate commerce to knowingly attempt to induce an individual under eighteen to engage in criminal sexual activity.

Count Two: *18 USC. § 2252(a)(4)(b). 2* Knowingly possessing one or more visual depictions transmitted in interstate commerce by computer involving a minor engaging in sexually explicit conduct.

In 2008, a federal judge had very little leeway in sentencing. The Guidelines, a set of sentencing rules passed in 1984, removed almost all of a federal judge's discretion. The Guidelines were part of a well-intentioned attempt to make federal sentences more uniform across the country. Before the Guidelines, judges were expected to fashion a sentence that was fair and satisfied both the societal goals of punishment and rehabilitation.

The Guidelines changed that. The result was a spreadsheet of levels, sentencing ranges, and factors in aggravation and mitigation that rejected the thoughtful analysis of an experienced judge in favor of a mechanical calculation. The Guidelines gave rise to rampant abuse of the system.

Every federal crime had a level, and that level equated to the range of months of the prison sentence. Judges could vary from that range only by "departing" from the Guidelines. Departures consisted of recognized reason to either increase (aggravate) or decrease (mitigate) the sentence. Factors in aggravation and mitigation were listed in the Guidelines, and only those factors listed could be considered.

The Guidelines prescribed enhancements for many crimes, but drug offenses and sex crimes involving children—even in cases where no contact had taken place—had been subject to such draconian enhancements that they created an outcry not just among defendants and criminal defense attorneys but also among federal judges themselves. The Guidelines remain a hot-button constitutional issue ("cruel and unusual punishment") with thousands of defendants sentenced to decades of enhancements piled onto already onerous prison terms. In New York, Illinois, and California, for example, district judges have gone on record complaining that mandatory sentencing stripped them of discretionary powers, particularly the power to extend mercy.

In Stan's case, in addition to the base sentence, each

count had possible enhancements listed as well, factors like the age and handicap of the victim and whether the defendant had exhibited a pattern of activity related to his criminal behavior.

But the well-intentioned effort to ensure uniformity resulted in ridiculous unfairness during its reign. For that reason, the Guidelines are now advisory rather than mandatory. Few cases illustrated the unfairness of the Guidelines more than *United States v. Stanley G. Rothenberg*.

Stan was a sixty-four-year-old man with no prior criminal record who had never touched a child. Not only had he never touched "Wayne's" child, the child didn't even exist, much less was under the age of twelve or handicapped. She was purely the figment of one cop's imagination and the details deftly crafted to play on the rigidity and weaknesses in the Guidelines.

Both Stan's felonies carried "pattern of activity" enhancements, which can be argued—or twisted from a defendant's perspective—by an adept prosecutor. Count One entails *a pattern* of "prohibited sexual conduct." Count Two *a pattern* of "sexual abuse or exploitation of a minor."

"This happened one time," Stan insisted, "over one twenty-four-hour period of phone calls and chats with one undercover cop involving one imaginary child."

He was convinced that this was the total extent of his lawbreaking. That's why he hired high-flying, high-priced, well-connected lawyers Michael Metz and Richard Lubin.

"I told myself all I had to do was have a little more patience and things would work themselves out," he recalled. "I felt that they would hire the best expert witnesses and build the best possible defense. I never gave up hope that I would survive this case."

Inevitably, Stan's thoughts returned to the printed-out chats that the police confiscated from his condo. Like his video porn collection, the chats were overwhelmingly homosexual erotica—bluntly put, fodder for masturbatory fantasies. Still, Stan insisted, they were outrageous sexual fantasies, not crimes of commission. However, in the hands of a zealous prosecutor, the most egregious chats and a telltale thumb drive containing ninety-seven images of child porn were ticking time bombs.

Conceivably, Judge Graham could send him to prison for thirty-four years even with a guilty plea. "No way," he assured himself after running worst case scenarios in his head. "No way!"

■ ■ ■

The Presentence Report being prepared by the probation office loomed over his head like the blade of doom. In the weeks leading up to his sentencing, his defense team rushed to marshal and prep expert witnesses and to pore over testimony and depositions to buttress his case. Judge Graham relentlessly drove things forward, ordering a written summary of the defense's expert testimony in hand forty-five days before sentencing, allowing the prosecution to counter. They were required to share their experts seven days prior to the sentencing hearing.

Metz and Lubin planned to seek a downward departure from the Guidelines based on Stan's good character and pristine record. Stan's lifetime rap sheet consisted of a few traffic violations. He also had a long history of volunteerism and community service and an extensive and very well-documented history of severe anxiety and depression, which may or may not have been linked to his blocking problems.

On September 4, as part of the defense's strategy, Dr. William Samek, a forensic psychologist (a specialist working at the intersection of psychology and the law) and director of the Florida Sexual Abuse Treatment Program, interviewed Stan at the Palm Beach County Jail. As part of this encounter, Samek administered a battery of tests, including the Minnesota Multiphasic Personality Inventory-2 (MMPI). To assess the likelihood of Stan engaging in future criminal behavior—a critical factor in a sentencing hearing—Samek used two other standard assessment tools: Hanson's Rapid Risk Assessment for Sex Offense Recidivism and Epperson's Minnesota Sex Offender Screening Tool (MnSOST).

The MMPI, a widely used measure of adult personality and psychopathology, provided a startlingly precise picture of Stan's psyche: a man experiencing acute distress (not surprising), who tended to be depressed, nervous, tense, unhappy, and worried; an individual who manifested numerous physical complaints and symptoms; a person who relied on denial and repression to deal with anxiety and other painful and debilitating feelings.

The MMPI profile suggested Stanley Rothenberg was an individual who "tends to be quite sensitive, somewhat passive, and compliant in interpersonal relationships." He had trouble with confrontations and expressing anger, problems with concentration and memory, difficulties making decisions. Those fitting this profile were convinced their health was failing and have numerous medical concerns. They experience emotions more intensely than others, feel lonely and misunderstood, are passive-dependent in relationships, and easily hurt. Fearing rejection, they avoid confrontation.

This was not the portrait of a predator.

Dr. Samek concluded that Stanley Rothenberg would "never likely pose a threat to children." His diagnosis was based on his interviews and an assessment of more than two dozen risk factors. Among Samek's findings:

Stan was not minimizing his behaviors or his problems.

He demonstrated the ability to develop psychological insight.

He had the ability to modify his behaviors.

He had never been arrested for committing a sexual offense before.

His sexual interest in children was more voyeuristic than hands-on.

His sexual interest was implemented by proxy. Stan talked to adults, not children, about molesting children.

It was not clear whether he would have followed through on what he fantasized and planned with Detective Spector—the crime for which Spector arrested him.

Stan clearly had ambivalent feelings about what he was considering.

His scores on the Static–99, RRASOR, and MnSOST-R, instruments designed to predict the likelihood of recidivism, were extremely low.

Michael Metz buttressed Stan's case with a twenty-three-page 2004 Social Security Administration (SSA) ruling that declared him fully disabled and awarded Stan retroactive disability benefits; a finding based on a confirmed diagnosis of "major depressive disorder, generalized anxiety disorder, and spinal stenosis (a narrowing of the spinal canal characterized by pain, numbness, paresthesia, and loss of motor control)."

To make his case, Stan provided the SSA with detailed medical and psychological histories including hospitalizations tied to his attempt to kick his long-term benzodiazepine dependency and lifelong blocking problems. After rounds of bureaucratic wrangling and reversal, an SSA panel decided that Stan was fully disabled. This ruling was critical to Metz's strategy for convincing Judge Graham that the facts warranted a downward departure from the Guidelines.

The defense lawyers marshalled other arguments for mitigation: the recidivism rate among aging sex offenders like Stan was miniscule; his arrest and prosecution (he made headlines in Florida newspapers and on TV) had been public and punitive; as a sex offender he was a marked man and would endure a shame – and guilt-ridden existence – for the rest of his life; the enduring trauma he suffered going through cold turkey benzodiazepine withdrawal in a jail cell; the dismantling and destruction of a life that had been heretofore unblemished, even exemplary. All were painful lessons and punishments that Stanley Rothenberg was never, ever likely to forget.

■　■　■

Stan's future was a chess game. He was a pawn. On October 16, Prosecutor Rinku Talwar, every inch a match for Metz and Lubin, countered their expert witnesses with a medical expert of her own: University of South Florida psychiatrist Wade Cooper Meyers. She moved that Dr. Meyers conduct a clinical interview with Stan "to adequately respond to the defendant's claims." Michael Metz could only stipulate that a member of his defense team attend the interview. Judge Graham granted the motion.

Additionally, Talwar wanted access to the dozens of underlying documents and records that SSA administrative law judges Marcos Rodriguez and Jose Rolon-Rivera used to determine Stan's disability. She homed in on Judge Rodriguez's findings that Stan made "inconsistent statements which raise doubt as to his credibility." The SSA balked, but on October 23, Judge Graham ordered Stan to authorize the release of his records.

■ ■ ■

By the numbers: on Count One, the Guidelines determined Stan's adjusted "offense level" as thirty-nine, plus a five-level enhancement for a pattern of activity "involving prohibited sexual conduct." He was granted a three-level reduction for accepting responsibility and having no criminal history. His offense level tallied forty-one. (By comparison, murder was assigned a forty-three.)

The math was simple and stark. Stan was facing 324 to 405 months in prison on one count, twenty-seven to thirty-four years.

On Count Two, Stan's offense level was thirty-three, plus a five-level enhancement for a pattern of activity "involving the sexual abuse or exploitation of a minor." The evidence for that "pattern" was the box of chat printouts police discovered in Stan's condominium.

Despite the possible sentence, Stan was cautiously optimistic. He knew—and felt that it was completely obvious to everyone—that he was not nearly the monster they claimed. He'd never touched the child, never engaged in any abusive contact with a child. At most, he had some dirty pictures of children on a thumb drive, and he'd talked dirty to a cop. Surely once he got in front of the judge and could explain it all, everything would be straightened out. Judges were educated and experienced;

they weren't lying cops trying to trap otherwise good citizens. The judge would do the right things.

"I put my life in the hands of Judge Graham," Stan later said. "I felt cautiously optimistic that I'd get below the ten-year minimum. I had to believe that. Otherwise, there was the thought I'd die in prison and never see the light of day again. I knew I had been a model citizen for sixty-four years and that I was inherently a good person.

"Surely, all of this would surely come out in my sentencing hearing."

Stan was sentenced to 300 months in prison.

In contrast, former Speaker of the House and serial molester Dennis Hastert, a man who had actually molested children, was sentenced to fifteen months.

Twelve

STAN ROTHENBERG'S TENURE with the US Public
Health Service was coming to a close. Bored, and subject
to episodes of blocking despite being on antianxiety medication, he felt like generations of frustrated public servants
before him: he was trapped in a low-paying, dead-end job
where advancement was skewed, unpredictable, or outright biased. In any event, the PHS was always a stopgap,
a temporary detour on the road to a real job and career.
Deciding to wing it, he handed in his resignation.

Fate works in strange ways.

A week later, Stan was invited to dinner at his neighbor
Jerry Effron's apartment on Southwest 27th Avenue. There
he was introduced to David Jacks, a striking young man
who'd recently moved to Florida. Instantly, Stan and David
were checking each other out, but it didn't feel like another
potential sexcapade or casual friendship. It felt real. As if by
magic, Stanley Rothenberg's secret dream of a caring, long-
term relationship was right in front of him.

The rounds of casual sexual encounters came to a screeching halt. Stan was still insecure and anxious, but falling in love transformed him.

Stan and Dave were polar opposites. Stan, at twenty-five, was 6'5", shy, inner-directed, frugal, practical, at a loss with anything mechanical; David, twenty-two, was a displaced California surfer, 5'10", well-built, artistic, hands-on, good with tools, happy to tinker and fix and build. He was working as a telephone installer for Southern Bell, scampering up telephone poles (Stan was acrophobic), wiring in switching units, and chatting up housewives.

The eldest of three boys, David was born in San Jose, California, to Betty, an office worker, and Wilbur, a handyman with a drinking problem. Wilbur was absent for much of David's life; Betty barely made ends meet working at the city of Mountain View's Water and Sewer Services. She depended on David to look after the younger siblings, Eddie and Artie. He did that and more, working part-time jobs to supplement the family income, cooking, cleaning, overseeing his brothers' schoolwork, and keeping them out of mischief.

On weekends, Betty was home to watch his younger brothers. David and his buddies strapped their surfboards to the top of his '61 Chevy and headed down Highway 101 to the beach, Jan and Dean and The Beach Boys blasting on the radio.

David graduated from high school in 1965. He had a penchant for design but no idea how to pursue an artistic career. He was a working-class kid, and there was no mentor or guidance counselor at his high school to show him the way forward. The Vietnam conflict was escalating under Lyndon Johnson. David enrolled at San Jose

State, mostly to avoid the draft, commuted back and forth to look after his brothers, and worked many hours in a sandwich shop. Sexually, David was far more experienced than Stan was. Even in his teens, David was sneaking off to nearby parks for quickie encounters. As for college, he barely lasted a semester.

Unlike Stan, sexually conflicted and repressed as a teen, David embraced his homosexuality (though he didn't broadcast it; no one did in that era). Growing up in laid-back northern California was a factor, but David was, by nature and instinct, confident, seductive, and free-wheeling.

"He'd known about being gay since he was in middle school," Stan recalled. "He readily discovered the places in San Jose where he could be solicited for a quickie or an hour's afternoon delight. David enjoyed being picked up in a mall bathroom or street corner by older men."

David's younger years were a stark contrast to Stan's complex, tortured adolescence in an overachieving, conservative family in Richmond, a place—like the rest of the Old South—where homosexuality was condemned as both a crime and a sin.

"David was the love of my life," Stan said in 2016. "With him still in my life, none of the rest would have happened."

David did hide that he was gay from his mother. Not unusual as the closet was crowded to overflowing in that era.

"He would have done anything for her," Stan explained. "He didn't want her to be ashamed of him. Or worse, reject him. In the '60s, for guys like us, it was better just to ignore the subject as long as you could."

When David dropped out of college, the draft and a precarious year-long tour in Vietnam were no longer clouds on a distant horizon. It was a real, even likely, possibility. David chose another, safer path; he enlisted in the US Coast Guard for a two-year tour. After he completed basic training, he was assigned to a Coast Guard cutter and shipped out. Onboard, he befriended an easy-going Southern guy with an affinity for bluegrass music. By some remarkable coincidence, it was Bob Zentz, the same hootenanny-loving, banjo-strumming Zentz who was Stan Rothenberg's roommate at William & Mary.

After his discharge, David returned to California and was relieved to learn that his mom had remarried. No longer held back by the need to be family protector and caretaker, he was free to follow whatever path in life he chose.

David nixed returning to San Jose State. His GI education benefits would cover only part of his tuition and fees, and besides, he had been there, done that. He'd seen a piece of the larger world in the service and like so many men and women in the Age of Aquarius, he was eager for new experiences, travel, adventure, and sex. The rock band, Steppenwolf, captured precisely what David was feeling in their anthem to rebellion, "Born to Be Wild."

■ ■ ■

Once again, fate played a role. A Coast Guard shipmate now living in a new high-rise apartment in Miami, Florida, invited David to move in with him. As Stan later recalled, "David gave the invite some thought and figured, 'Why not?' The guy was gay so he'd be David's intro into the Miami gay lifestyle. David also knew the guy was secretly in love with him, but that didn't really matter. The sheer anticipation of starting a new life was electric."

David packed up his new Mustang Fastback purchased

with money saved while he was the service, and headed out on the highway, east on I–10 to Miami, 3,000 miles away, to start a new life.

■ ■ ■

Two months later, on April 1, he met Stan at Jerry Effron's apartment. Electricity crackled. Either his insecurity or his proper Southern roots showing, Stan quickly proposed that they live together as lovers and partners. Eight days after they met, on April 10, 1969, Dave moved his few possessions into Stan's one-bedroom garden apartment in Coral Gables

As it turned out, David's preference was "bottom" to Stan's "top." According to Stan, the sex was hot and heavy, but there was romance there, as well as the beginnings of commitment evidenced in respect and affection. In an era of freewheeling sexuality and faithlessness, the two would spend twenty-four years of their lives together.

"When I met Stan," Jerry Effron recalled, "I noticed he was very protective of his feelings. I could tell something was wrong. I think he'd been hurt early in life. He used this biting, off-the-cuff humor to hide his true feelings. And then when he met David, I'd never seen such a positive, loving transformation in my life. I know a lot of people who have relationships, but this was one beautiful, fantastic, giving relationship. Love brought both of them to higher levels."

This closed-off aspect of Stan's personality was a recurrent theme among Stan's friends. Fred Halper said there were mysteries surrounding his friend he had never fully understood. "I'm still wondering what drove this warm, friendly, needy guy into this kind of a chat room…to the dark side," Halper said.

■ ■ ■

The unemployed Stan happily assumed most of the domestic responsibilities. David reported for work at the phone company at 7:30 a.m. Stan usually made him lunch, typically peanut butter and jelly sandwiches, potato chips, and fresh fruit, occasionally switching to egg salad or cold cut sandwiches. Both men were, by nature, frugal to the point of penny-pinching. They were also eager to build a nest egg, a trait that would serve them well in the future.

Like all eager young couples, they decided to spruce up Stan's tiny apartment. At Home Depot, they purchased boxes of stick-on gray plastic brick-and-mortar tiles that they applied to the space above and below the kitchen cabinets.

"We wanted to make it look like we were outside," Stan recalled. "It was very cheesy, but David and I felt that we'd just earned degrees in interior design."

Years later, when they owned a premier furniture store, they'd look back on their decorating choices then and laugh.

■ ■ ■

Of course, at the time, gay men could not even dream of marrying. In the streets of many towns and cities, they were derided as queers and harassed and persecuted, often violently.

But Stan was looking to the future, and he foresaw a brighter day. He decided his parents and siblings must come to terms with his sexuality and by extension, David. The choice was clear: accept Stan for who he was and who he loved, or lose him forever.

Two months after meeting David, he decided the time had come to have that vital conversation with Joe and Mollie Rothenberg. If things went wrong, he wouldn't be the first gay man ostracized from a family he loved.

"The plan was I'd go back to Virginia and tell my parents the truth about David and me," he recalled. "If my mother resisted, I'd return to Miami and search for employment somewhere. If she understood the intensity of our relationship, the plan was that both of us would move to Richmond. I'd work for my dad in his Shockoe Bottom furniture store. David would use his GI benefits to attend Virginia Commonwealth University and study art."

Arriving back in Richmond, Stan waited for the right moment to break the news to his mother. (His dad would remain in the dark until things settled down.)

Late one evening, he was lying in bed in his old bedroom and Mollie was sitting on the edge of the bed. They were talking about his plans for the future, about his life in Florida. Stan felt the anxiety rising but his love for David tamped it down.

When he could no longer stand the waiting, he came out and just said it. "David is more than a roommate to me; he is my sex partner."

Stan remembered Mollie, always so rational and unemotional, sitting on the edge of the bed trying to process what the hell her son was saying. Mollie was momentarily speechless, her brow stretched smooth as a drumhead.

"Then in her cerebral, inimitable way," Stan recalled, "she said she wanted to 'go to the public library to read up on this (homosexuality) thing.' I believe nascent guilt was much more in play than any feeling that my relationship was icky. She was not turned off by my words, but mystified by the 'why' question."

Perhaps at some level, his secret was no secret at all, and he'd just confirmed her long-held suspicion.

After a while, she made up her mind. "Mother seemed pleased that we'd be coming to Richmond," Stan recalled. "She told me she'd broach the subject with Dad in a week or so. Fortunately, my dad had no problem with both of us living together and my working for him."

Joe and Mollie may have been unfamiliar with homosexuality but they were not naive. Like most parents, they would have preferred Stan travel a less arduous path in life. There would be no wedding, no Bar Mitzvahs for grandsons sprung from his loins, but there was fear, always the fear, that something terrible would befall him. They loved Stan and wanted the best for him. Fortunately, they didn't live to see the fear that something would happen come to fruition.

Late in August 1969, as Stan put together excuses to break his apartment lease, a quarter of a million long-haired Aquarians were streaming into upstate New York for "Three Days of Peace and Music," the Woodstock Festival. Stan, a bit older and more conservative, was not a part of that raucous world. He had even convinced David to part with his beloved Mustang Fastback because it was impractical. Instead, they packed up Stan's green, four-door Rambler Rebel in the blistering heat and headed north, laughing and joking on I-95, the sparkle of downtown Miami's glass towers reflected in the rear-view mirror.

Stan went to work for his father at the Richmond furniture store. Joe Rothenberg was successful, but he worked hard for his living, and the store was no showcase.

"An old, one-story building without central heating or hot water, just a toilet and basic electricity," Stan recalled. "Dad had a coal – and wood-burning stove in the back of the building. Once a week during the winter, I'd drive to a Hungerford Coal outlet and purchase twenty-five bags of coal. It was a dirty business. On a very cold day, getting the heat going would take three or four hours."

Stan wrestled sofas and refrigerators, bedroom sets, and electric stoves onto delivery trucks dispatched all over Richmond, not exactly the fast lane to success he'd imagined. "I wasn't afraid of work, but I was not a hands-on guy," he remembered. "I had to be shown what to do. I had the credentials for a white-collar job but didn't know which one. I did know I wasn't going to be doing manual labor for the rest of my life!"

But while manual labor may not have been his forte, he was also learning the ins and outs of the retail furniture business: purchasing, receiving, sales, marketing, credit transactions, managing costs, and boosting profits, a hardcore education in the realities of business. This would prove a critical part of their future.

David was also getting an education, one that involved less manual labor. He applied and was accepted into the Virginia Commonwealth University (VCU) baccalaureate program as a painting and printmaking major.

Stan and David rented a modest duplex apartment in Richmond's Fan District on one of the tree-lined streets radiating outward from the campus. It was a typical late-'60s college enclave, populated by students, untenured faculty members, struggling artists, hippies, gays, and political activists, a whiff of counterculture—and marijuana—in an overwhelmingly conservative, but not oppressive, Southern city. For the next two years, they

lived, as Stan recalled, "as newlyweds would," setting out
for work and school in the morning, dividing household
responsibilities, spending lots of time alone and lots of
time in the bedroom. Now it was David's turn to run the
house. Arriving home early, he shopped and prepared
"real dinners—entrees and salads and vegetables."

Stan took care of the bills, bought the insurance policies, assembled a modest suite of furniture, and handled
all the mundane tasks of apartment living. When the
downstairs tenant's barking dog drove them to distraction
in the mornings, it was Stan who approached him and
complained to the landlord.

One night, while Stan and David were at a movie, a
squad of Richmond vice cops acting on a faulty or mali-
cious tip broke into their apartment allegedly searching
for drugs. Neither man was a recreational drug user. The
invasion so outraged Stan that he wrote an angry letter
to US Senator Sam Ervin—later of Watergate fame—complaining that their constitutional rights had been violated.
Ervin dutifully entered the letter into the Congressional
Record. The incident, if not a watershed moment, was
very significant for Stan: he became energized politically,
focusing primarily on gay rights, but also race relations,
human rights, and social justice. Given his personality,
Stan was hardly a firebrand, but he would be politically
active and socially involved for most of his life.

By the end of their second year in Richmond, Stan and
David had saved enough money for a down payment on
a home. They settled on a nondescript brick townhouse
bordering the VCU campus at 108 North Morris Street.
With the backing of a local mortgage lender—Home Beneficial—they bought it for $16,500, financed at 8 percent.
the house was owned by Mr. Van Cleef, once an assistant

principal at Stan's high school. Soon after, David brought home a kitten, and the family unit was complete.

They hired a well-known gay architect to draw up plans for a total renovation. He recommended a pair of skilled, gay-friendly woodworkers—Gregory Banducci and his partner, Harry—to handle the work. Stan and David continued to live in the house during the renovations and the loss of privacy was inevitable. Workers were there at all hours, and, "They'd run across some gay porn," Stan recalled. "Or maybe hear David and I having passionate sex."

What might have been unacceptable to a young heterosexual couple living in close quarters with strangers didn't bother Stan and David. They brought with them from Miami the uninhibited radical culture of sex. Sex and all things sexual were the pivot points of Stan and David's existence, as natural and normal as breathing. It would remain so for the rest of their lives.

One year later, they were the proud owners of a jewel box domicile: a bright, airy house with a state-of-the-art kitchen complete with hand-wrought hardwood countertops, an outsized living room, and a spiral staircase with treads of inlaid walnut. The gorgeous fifty-five-year-old house was included in the Fan Civic Association's 1974 Christmas House Tour. There was a sour note: David's name could not be included in the house tour's brochure as Stan's partner. A straight unmarried couple would have no such problem—another of the thousand indignities gay men had to endure.

"Now our home was totally contemporary," Stan recalled, "but where do we find contemporary furnishings in totally traditional Richmond?"

Joe Rothenberg's low-end merchandise was unsuitable

and the only downtown store offering contemporary pieces was poorly stocked. They had no choice but to pick and choose from what was available through mail-order catalogs. The process was endlessly frustrating, but the experience was priceless.

■ ■ ■

Emboldened by the success of his letter to Senator Ervin—Stan never forgot that he was in the Congressional Record—Stan ventured into community activism. Since VCU had no dedicated parking facility, VCU students' cars were packed into every residential street in the Lower Fan District, leaving no space for the residents to park. Stan, a stickler for procedures, dutifully wrote his city councilman, who contacted a university counterpart, who eventually answered with the council's standard answer: there was no money for a parking deck. An umbrella civic organization—the Fan Civic Association—was equally unresponsive.

Stalemate.

Stan canvassed the neighborhood, handing out fliers and organizing meetings, until he had enough support to organize a Lower Fan Civic Association. Stan was elected the first president. He haunted recalcitrant community board members and city council meetings, fired off letters, and networked with other activists on other issues and concerns.

It took two years, but the parking problem was finally resolved: stickers were issued to neighborhood residents. The victory was the beginning of three decades of gratifying, often meaningful, community activism and service.

■ ■ ■

On weekends, Stan and David joined other gay men on the pilgrimage to the Dial Tone on West Cary Street, a popular gay bar. The place was owned by a reputed organized crime figure named Leo Khoury, who happily lived up to his unsavory reputation. In the Fan District, the Dial Tone was the only place for gay men to socialize, drink, and wriggle on the tiny dance floor. Its previous incarnation—Rathskellers—was shut down by the Virginia Alcoholic Control Board for allegedly "serving too many gays." Since it was technically illegal to serve alcohol to "known homosexuals," Khoury undoubtedly had an arrangement with the vice squad to look the other way. In return, he charged his hapless clientele extortionate prices. It was pretty much the same story in every gay community in the country.

In 1969, harassment and brutality by the NYPD triggered the infamous Stonewall riots on Christopher Street in Manhattan's West Village. In gay culture, the Stonewall riots were roughly equivalent to the original Tea Party and Bunker Hill, the opening volley for the Gay Liberation Movement.

Stan and David became friendly with a neighborhood couple, Dottie and Carolyn, taking turns hosting potluck dinners and card games. The women were handy "beards" whenever the two guys need "straight dates" at social events in staid Richmond. After Carolyn moved on to a fun-loving outdoorsy woman named Andrea, the foursome took a memorable camping trip to Virginia Beach in a pop-up trailer. Entertaining and ever resourceful, David handled the cooking on a portable two-burner gas stove as the klutzy Stan ("I can't handle anything more complicated than tying my shoes") looked on in admiration. They spend a riotous—and to Stan, terrifying—night tumbled on top of each other as the camper was buffeted and rocked by a powerful thunderstorm. The morning dawned crystal clear, the sun warm, the sky a mesmerizing blue, not even a cloud on the horizon.

Life was good. Stan had David, a lovely home, a steady job, and his family. There was no reason to suspect that anything would shatter that idyllic state of affairs.

Thirteen

1975
Richmond, Virginia

WHAT WAS PERFECT and idyllic for Stan wasn't enough for David, who remembered the frothy and flamboyant sexual environment of Miami—and missed it. Unbeknownst to the staid and monogamous Stan, David reverted to the street hustling of his teens, not for money this time, but for the raw thrill of anonymous sex. Slipping off one afternoon, he cruised the leafy paths and overgrown dells of Byrd Park, north of the James River, a notorious spot for gay liaisons.

As Stan later explained, "David propositioned the wrong guy, an undercover vice cop."

Back in the day, law enforcement agents referred to these stings as "bag-a-fag" operations. Richmond's notorious anti-solicitation ordinance targeted homosexual men more than female hookers—in particular young gays cruising the parks and downtown streets around the library, older chicken hawks preying on working-class teens who'd sell their bodies for a few dollars, and married suburbanites of dubious sexuality who drove station wagons around the library eager for a quickie encounter before returning home to the wife and kids.

Ironically, the law's sponsor, Stan insisted, was a closeted city councilman named Raymond R., who ran a successful car dealership in the Ninth Ward, a conservative blue-collar area on the south side of the James River. Any hapless homosexual arrested in Richmond in those years found himself outed over breakfast in the *Richmond Times Dispatch.* Amazingly, the situation persisted in Virginia's capital almost a decade after the Stonewall riots and the birth of the gay liberation movement in the United States.

Virginia still treats gays as second-class citizens. Richmond's "cruising statute" is apparently still on the books, though the state's "crimes against nature" laws (one prohibits oral sex between heterosexual couples) had been declared unconstitutional. (In 2000, the state court of appeals [*Elvis Gene DePriest, et al. v. Commonwealth* of *Virginia*] ruled that "individuals charged with solicitation to commit sodomy have not established a presumption of privacy by seeking to commit sodomy in a public park.")

■ ■ ■

In Richmond, Stanley Rothenberg and David Jacks, both publicly out of the closet, were known as upright citizens steadfastly making their way into the business community and participating in the city's seemingly-Byzantine social structure. With David's arrest, all this respectability was in jeopardy. A nervous Stan retained Murray J. Janus, one of the city's top criminal defense lawyers. Janus advised David to put himself under psychiatric care, which he did. (An insight into how gay men were viewed.) Upon completion of treatment and bearing an official letter certifying that he was now "rehabilitated," David was permitted to plead guilty to a misdemeanor and thus avoid jail time. Stan later said the interlude cost them "a pretty penny."

Rather than anger, jealousy, and recrimination, David's arrest became what Stan would later call a watershed moment: "It precipitates a discussion about our having an open relationship." In those years, that very same conversation was underway among numerous straight couples, but for gay men, whether in committed relationships, casually dating, or unattached, the floodgates were opened.

"This was all new to me and the beginning of an era of sexual promiscuity by both of us," Stan remembered.

Now liberated, Stan made it a point to walk over to Virginia Commonwealth University where a brisk trade in quickies was underway in the bathroom stalls. Hesitant, despite himself, he mostly returned home unsatisfied.

Stan said, "It was not unusual for us to drive up to an industrial building in southeast DC and check into the Club Washington (one of a national chain of Club Baths) for about three to four hours of fun and frolic, and drive back home in the wee hours of the morning."

Not surprisingly, the bathhouse, a bricked-up beige warehouse, was in a very dicey neighborhood, so dicey that off-duty policemen were hired to provide security. At the time, no one noticed or cared but condom use was a rarity.

Many years later, Stan tried to put the reckless encounters in historical context. "Anonymous sex was something that gay men engage in because society refuses to stamp our lifestyle as normal, with expectations and rules to abide by," he said. "Since we have no rules, no behavior was off the table. Let me add that, in the '70s and early '80s, gays had never heard of HIV. The worst we thought we could get was syphilis or the clap."

To their shame, many doctors who were gay reinforced this notion. They, too, were part of this new, make-it-up-as-you-go-along gay culture. The growing hepatitis B epidemic, which became a marker for the spread of HIV, was ignored, along with an explosive increase in other STDs among the gay male population. A new medical term was actually coined—gay bowel syndrome—which diagnosticians used when they discovered unwanted microbes in unexpected places.

The HIV and AIDS epidemic had not yet occurred. The emotional and psychological bill of a culture that downplayed monogamy (and the virtues of commitment, loyalty, and emotional love) and elevated hedonism had yet to be presented. It was precisely the argument that sex was free, elemental and beneficial, sacramental—the communion of the gay "church"—that would prove not only unsustainable, but catastrophic. (By 2010, thirty years after the epidemic was first discovered, AIDs had claimed more than 636,000 lives, the majority gay or bisexual men. In 2016, a million Americans were percolating the virus, the majority still gay or bisexual men.)

Even when the gay cultured changed, even as AIDS ravaged the gay community, Stan would remain thoroughly and permanently acculturated, a "church member," sex-driven and lustful long after his youth faded and his hungers and yearnings were purely fantasy. David and Stan, avatars of this culture, remained a couple, living and working and sleeping together into the '90s, as the world shifted around them. It was their failure to move on from the frantic sex-fueled days in Miami that eventually led Stan into the dark world of AOL's FamilyLuv—and from there, to prison.

Fourteen

STAN AND DAVID spent that summer quietly at the annual Rothenberg family gathering. "For decades, my mother arranged to rent a condo at Virginia Beach," Stan recalled. "All the Rothenbergs, including spouses, were invited—expected—to be in attendance. David and I drive down for about a week."

The gathering was a milestone in Stan's life. Six years earlier, he'd taken a stand: he wanted to bring David, his partner and lover, to accompany him to the beach.

"Mother and I talked about it," Stan's sister, Gail Lewis, recalled in 2015. "We knew he was gay. We knew he and Dave lived together. We just didn't want to see them being affectionate. It was 'Keep your distance.'"

All the Rothenberg brothers, wives, children, and significant others were already en route. "That's when Stan put his foot down," Gail continued. "He basically said, 'Love me, love Dave.'" What might have been an uncomfortable and unsettling encounter comes off smoothly and graciously. "Dave brought Mother flowers," Gail added. "We really got to know him. He was such a great person that he was quickly and absolutely accepted into our family." She paused, trying to control a flood of tears. "You know I really admired Stan for his courage."

As the years passed, the other Rothenberg siblings were pulled in different directions by life's challenges—divorce, dysfunction, career demands, and physical distance. It was the parents—Joe and Mollie—and Stan and David who remained the constants in the family photo albums.

■ ■ ■

On a rainy afternoon during that 1976 beach vacation, Stan and David decided to have a "look-see" at a store they'd heard about—Danish Furniture Fair—on West 21st Street in Norfolk. When they arrived, they were astounded at the quality and variety of the showroom collection.

"All the items were contemporary, unique, practical, and oh-so-sleek, the kind of furniture we've always wanted," Stan recalled. "Teak and Brazilian Rosewood, Dansk pendant lamps, fabrics, and dining room table runners designed by famous artists. We stand there drooling, trying to figure out how to get a whole houseful of this stuff into a four-door Rambler."

By the time a salesperson appeared, lightbulbs were going off in their heads. Given Stan's background and David's artistic flair—their love for all that was sleek and modern and tasteful—this could be an opportunity. They would open a store of their own.

After a hastily arranged meeting, the Danish-born owner—Claus Ihlemann—agreed to supply Stan and

David with inventory from his warehouse, priced at wholesale, plus a 15 percent markup.

Rather than attempting the daunting complexities of importing and shipping, taxes and duties, all they'd have to do to get started was drive a hundred miles to Norfolk and stock up. "I could hardly contain my excitement," Stan remembered. "David was the lynchpin of the concept because he'd be the one to do all the interior design work, create the ads, and ready the store for business. I'd handle the back end of the business."

Within a year, Scandinavian Interiors opened for business across the street from Joe Rothenberg's Shockoe Bottom operation. With a little financial help from Dad and a new '77 Ford pickup, the two newly-minted entrepreneurs were underway. Frugal to begin with, they spent the next five years pinching every penny, putting what they saved into upgrading the showroom, expanding offerings via catalogs, boosting advertising, and monitoring the exchange rate to save a few Danish and Norwegian krone.

By 1980, they were doing well enough to secure the landlord's permission to break through a wall and expand into a vacant building next door, increasing their floor space by half. David exposed brick and installed handmade spotlights (constructed out of vegetable cans) and other decor elements; Stan busied himself mastering the intricacies of duties, tariffs, import fees, and ocean and inland freight brokerage. They hired Bruce, their first employee, who not surprisingly happened to be gay.

By 1982, Scandinavian Interiors was so successful another expansion was in the works. "We're offering a unique product at a fair price in a city that had only one other contemporary furniture store," explained Stan. "Plus,

David and I were extremely complementary in terms of knowledge and ability. We work long hours at no pay to ensure a long-haul success."

On a tip from his father, Stan got a line on a two-story building—16,000 square feet—about to go on the market. The building was at 3117 West Cary Street, in the heart of Carytown, one of the city's hippest and most eclectic neighborhoods. It was air-conditioned and had elevators and four spectacular showcase windows looking out onto a bustling sidewalk. After much fretting, number-crunching, and huddling with attorneys and accountants, they closed the deal for $225,000.

Scandinavian Interiors opened its doors that spring. Stan and David were now suitably high-profile figures in Richmond to attract City Councilman Andrew Gillespie III to handle the ribbon-cutting ceremony.

Over the next years, sales and profits continued to soar. One of the pieces they showcased, the Balans Chair—more commonly known as an ergonomic kneeling chair—produced by a cutting-edge Norwegian design house, Westnofa, was in such demand it became a cult item.

In the spring of 1983, the two traveled to Norway on an all-expenses-paid junket underwritten by a consortium of furniture factories. The highlight of the trip, Stan recalled, was a ski excursion to Geilo, a resort town in the Hallingdal Valley northwest of Oslo.

At the time, Stan was thirty-nine years old; David was thirty-six. Neither one of them had ever strapped on snow skis. After one lesson, David, fearless and agile, was moving ahead full speed, executing maneuvers that left faint-hearted Stan flabbergasted. (He did, however, notice the handsome blond ski instructor.) Determined not to be left behind, Stan trudged up the mountain after David, who was so caught up in the adventure that he barely acknowledge his partner's presence.

"I feel a level of anxiety more intense than anything I'd experienced before going on benzo therapy," Stan recalled, describing the vertiginous downslope that laid before him. Between moments of utter panic and the invocation of Hebrew prayers half-remembered from his Bar Mitzvah, he somehow made it to the bottom without falling. It was a measure of Stan's continuing emotional fragility that, thirty-three years later, his memories of this terrifying, albeit short-lived, experience covered eight handwritten pages in his memoir.

On the ground, things were flowing much more smoothly. By the late 1980s, Scandinavian Interiors employed thirteen people and owned three delivery trucks. Its annual sales were climbing toward $1 million. Stan was now a board member of the Retail Merchants Association of Greater Richmond.

In short, Stanley Rothenberg and David Jacks, two hardworking, happy young men who happen to be gay, were well on their way to achieving the American dream.

With his business a success, Stan revisited his favorite pastime—baseball. He treated himself to two box seats at Parker Field, the Richmond Virginians' creaky, oft-flooded but venerable baseball stadium. Then he decided to sponsor an LGBT softball team, a historic first, in Richmond's Summer City League. Stan, a first baseman, paid for the team's uniforms, equipment, and other expenses for eight years.

"We were proud to be known as the LGBT team," he remembered. "We did experience some bullying at the start of most seasons, but it died down. It gave us great pleasure to defeat some of the 'macho' teams."

■ ■ ■

Even before he was a well-known businessman, Stan
continued his trend of community involvement. Shortly
after Stan moved back to Richmond in 1969, Hurricane
Camille slammed into the area, wreaking havoc. Three
years later, in 1972, Hurricane Agnes devastated coastal
North Carolina and Virginia, triggering massive flooding
in Richmond's low-lying Shockoe Bottom.

When Hurricane Agnes hit, the surging James River
overwhelmed a pumping station, driving floodwaters up
into the second floor of Joe Rothenberg's store. In the rest
of Shockoe Bottom, the flooding was so extensive that
many merchants simply pulled up stakes and moved. Two
major hurricanes in three years was too much.

Looking at the devastation, Stan's orderly mind recognized that much of it was preventable. With the proper
systems in place, the hurricane floodwaters could have
been held at bay. His orderly, frugal mind despaired at the
massive destruction that could have been prevented by
adequate infrastructure.

Stan joined the bureaucratic battle to save the neighborhood. He and Lester Blackiston, the Bottom's rowdy
and infamous character—poet, art collector, restaurateur,
and activist—formed the Shockoe Bottom Improvement
Association. Stan covered the organization's start-up costs.
The SBIA eventually put enough pressure on state legislators that the legislators signed off on the Army Corps
of Engineers' plan to construct manmade levees on both
banks of the James River.

By that time, Stan was a true political junkie. In a city
that once would have rejected him, that had laws against
his very existence, he was now a part of the community.

A leader, even. He made a difference in the world, he was recognized and honored for his service. For the lanky young man who'd fled to Miami to find himself, his newly-found respectability was something he treasured.

Stan made a point of attending the twice-a-month city council meetings, often staying past midnight when the sessions ran late. "I developed relationships with a number of members of the Council," he recalled. "When an ordinance came up for discussion that I felt a need to express my opinion, I walked up to the mic and spoke." For a man who'd been too terrified by social anxiety to even try out for a baseball team in college, this was a remarkable transformation.

By then, even the mayor knew who Stan was, recognition that would serve him in good stead. "I see myself as a people's advocate," Stan said, "who speaks for the poor and downtrodden."

His community involvement and commitment continued—with greater impact—now that he was an entrepreneur and chamber of commerce stalwart. "David and I were gay men who own our own business," Stan explained. "No one can extort money or really hurt us in any meaningful way. This was immensely liberating because there were still laws on the books that could ruin people's lives. Luckily, we have no problem being out."

This was still a time when the overwhelming majority of Richmond's gay community and business owners were in the closet. "We were unknown and inconspicuous," remembered Guy Kinman, a founder of Richmond's gay rights movement, "feeling our jobs and families were at risk if we were known. The stigma was so bad we wouldn't acknowledge each other in a public forum.

"Stan Rothenberg was different. He has always been a

hero to me because while gay people lived in the shadows, he was straightforward and treated everybody fairly. His reputation was as a businessman, someone who'd show up and speak his piece at the city council and on TV. You had to admire a man like that who was living with a nature that people seemingly abhor, but living quite a normal life—with a family he made with his partner and the outstanding family from which he came," Kinman said.

In 1979, the Richmond City Council appointed Stan to the city's Human Relations Commission. Though the commission was primarily focused on race relations, Stan, its first openly-gay member, used his influence to, "Bring to the forefront gross discrimination against gays and lesbians in private transactions, government employment, city contracts, public housing, and other areas of everyday life. Gays and lesbians had absolutely no protections, and I want to be the unofficial watchdog," he recalled. "At the time, this was the best I could hope for."

But over the next year, he realized that the commission and the pack of unenterprising local reporters covering its monthly meetings weren't interested in LGBT issues. His only ally was the commission chairman, Dr. Edward Peeples.

Finally, in 1984, in an effort to demonstrate that LGBT issues were significant and really deserved the commission's attention, Dr. Peeples took action. He commissioned a questionnaire to measure the level of discrimination felt by gay residents of Richmond.

"Most gay people had learned from bitter experience how to 'hide' their sexual orientation," Stan recalled. "Those who couldn't 'pass' took the mental and physical abuse dished out by the homophobes."

Energized, Stan spent weeks distributing the questionnaire in bars, bookstores, and coffee shops—all the familiar outposts of the gay community. The results, as Stan expected, detailed widespread bias and discrimination.

What he didn't expect was the ire of his fellow commissioners. "What I heard at our meetings," he recalled, "was pure hatred from people who were supposed to be open-minded about civil rights."

His fellow commissioners questioned the study's methodology; its reliability, validity, and even its legitimacy were challenged. Aside from Chairman Peeples, Stan was the only commissioner who advocated that sexual orientation be added to the city's human rights ordinance, in effect, making gays a protected class.

(This battle is still going on in the South. In 2016, North Carolina passed its so-called bathroom law, which restricts transgender people to the restroom facilities of their designated gender at birth and strips away statutes in Charlotte and Asheville that extend civil rights protection to gays.)

The Richmond study was assigned to a subcommittee for review. The meetings become so contentious, Stan found himself in furious shouting matches with a venomous and homophobic colleague named Robert Buerlein.

"Looking back, I realize that Mr. Buerlein's attacks really represented most Virginians' attitudes toward gay people at the time," Stan recalled. In the end, the commission declined to recommend the survey's findings to the full city council for discussion.

Stan considered running for a council seat. "I know lots of people in the Second Ward," he recalled, "but the bottom line was that I'm gay. I know that if it became a campaign issue I will lose automatically."

Bill Leidinger, the man who did run and won the seat

in the heavily gay ward, flat-out told Stan he would not sponsor or support a gay rights ordinance.

After six unsatisfying years on the Human Relations Commission, Stan stepped down in 1985, a "very disappointed man."

His political career was not yet over. He was offered a seat on the city council's new Crime Committee. Like so many 1980s-era initiatives, the committee was an attempt to come to grips with a devastating crack epidemic sweeping through American cities. It was persistent, low-grade lawlessness—muggings, purse snatching, burglaries, and car break-ins—quality of life crimes that propelled New York City Mayor Rudy Giuliani to fame when he ordered the NYPD to crack down and clean up the streets.

With Scandinavian Interiors growing almost exponentially, Stan no longer had much free time to devote to community service. Nonetheless, he dutifully spent a year at the Crime Committee's bi-weekly meetings, drafting reports and recommendations.

"Someone had to do it," he later said. "I worked hard and performed my civic duty to the best of my abilities."

Fifteen

THE DEADLY EPIDEMIC was coursing through America. Once labeled a "gay plague," AIDS was now in its seventh year, slowly and inevitably spreading among IV drug users, bisexuals, hemophiliacs, transfusion recipients, and their sexual partners. Film star Rock Hudson had died three years earlier; hemophiliac Ryan White, the AIDS poster boy ostracized by his Kokomo, Indiana, community was battling futilely for his life. Glaxo-Wellcome's AZT, the first FDA-approved anti-AIDS drug, was on the market, but at a price few patients could afford. An HIV screening test invented by virologist Robert Gallo was widely available. In 1988, about 4,900 Americans would die of the disease.

In America's devastated gay communities, a new subset—the worried well—emerged. These were men—Stan Rothenberg and David Jacks very much among them—who had engaged in anonymous sex with multiple high-risk partners in settings such as Key West,

Provincetown, Christopher Street, The Castro, Miami
Beach, Washington, DC, and Fire Island, and on beaches,
in bars, and in bathhouses that were known to be hotbeds
of transmission.

Both men were asymptomatic. David, ever the bolder
of the two, visited a clinic set up to provide anonymous
HIV testing. His blood was drawn on a Wednesday; the
results would be available in fourteen days.

Stan wanted no part of it.

"The thought of finding out that I might be positive
was terrifying," he recalled. "I couldn't handle the thought
of dying or finding out my soulmate was HIV-positive.
But this was David's decision."

Two weeks. Whatever inner turmoil he felt, David
stayed calm, almost nonchalant, matter-of-factly con-
fiding to the apprehensive Stan that he believed he was
infected. The day arrived, cool and sunny. David walked
out of his office, unlocked his maroon 1983 Saab, and
drove off to the clinic. Stan retreated to his second-floor
office to wait.

"I just want to crawl into a cave and forget everything,"
he remembered.

Forty-five minutes later, he watched as David pulled
into the parking lot at the back of the building, looking
for some sign.

A few minutes later, David opened the door to Stan's
office and walked in. He stood there not saying a word.

"His face was hard to read," Stan recalled, "but I get no
sense of good news. The moment was awkward and surreal. Finally. I break the silence and he whispers to me that
the test came back positive."

In such moments, the chasm between the healthy and
the unwell, the hopeful and those beyond hope, the living

and the dying is unbridgeable, no matter how deep the love, relationship, or connection that binds.

"How does one prepare to be told that your loved one, your soulmate, your business partner, your everything was now dying?" Stan asked many years later.

One of the most unsettling things about the HIV retrovirus is that a person can feel absolutely fine, completely healthy, for years, while unbeknownst, it is replicating and systematically destroying the immune system. HIV targets so-called T-helper cells, a subset of white blood cells that, in simple terms, orchestrate immune response. Unlike, for example, smallpox or Ebola, HIV doesn't kill. "Opportunistic infections"—pneumocystis pneumonia, Kaposi's sarcoma, toxoplasmosis, cryptosporidiosis, among them—eventually overwhelm an immuno-compromised victim. Even in the asymptomatic latent period, an infected person can spread the virus.

Thirty-five years of AIDS research (the disease was first detected in the US in 1981), has demonstrated that during anal sex, the virus was much less likely to pass from an HIV-positive receptive partner (bottom) to an insertive partner (top), numerically a one in 1,666 risk. Stan was a top. For the bottom, sex with an HIV-infected top, increases the risk of infection to one in 122. David was a bottom.

After David's diagnosis, Stan retreated into a psychological bunker. "David's test does not alter his health or condition; it just verified it," he said. "Yet my perception of reality was turned on its head. At the time, science did not know whether the virus was spread by casual contact, deep kissing, or some other way. These unknowns caused two people who dearly loved one another to literally avoid each other. We stopped sharing cups and eating food from the same plate. I did not feel comfortable kissing my partner on his lips. Our sex life was gone. All this happened so fast that it was too much to comprehend."

David's health remained stable for the next two years while he was on AZT, although he experienced most of the known side effects such as anemia, vomiting, headaches, fatigue, and muscle pain. Unfortunately, the antiretroviral AIDs cocktail, which dramatically reduces the morbidity and mortality of those infected with the virus, was four years away.

Stan and David decided to keep the news from the Scandinavian Interiors' staff. Most of them were gay men, undoubtedly facing tragedy and loss in their own lives. The last thing they needed was more anxiety and insecurity.

"HIV was causing chaos and grief for every gay male in America," Stan recalled. "I find myself opening the morning paper and immediately going to the obituary page."

He was not alone in this morbid obsession. In the *New York Times,* the obit page became a macabre guessing game, all these high-profile, successful, and talented young men dying inexplicably "after a long illness."

As 1990 wound to a close, the day-to-day strain, dread, and loss of focus were taking a toll. Scandinavian Interiors' profit margins were shrinking. Stan, though fretting over David, still refused to be tested.

"All our hard work means nothing. Our dreams for a nice retirement in a warm, sunny locale were shattered. David was a walking, ticking time bomb who one day will fall ill and die. It was not a question of if, but when."

In early 1991, Stan and David decided to shut down Scandinavian Interiors, their life's work. A going-out-of-business sale was set for March. With this, the employees could no longer be kept in the dark.

"The staff meeting was the most difficult I ever chaired," Stan recalled. "I could see tears welling up. I explain that David needs to travel the country while he was still healthy and enter any drug trials that offered hope."

A liquidator was brought in. The sale was a success. The dream was dead.

Unlike the majority of HIV/AIDS positive individuals, gay men, and IV drug users who were helpless before their fate, David had the will and financial resources to fight back against the disease. The cure was out there, David told himself, just out of reach. It was out there, and he would find it.

Before David departed, he accompanied Stan, who had finally worked up the courage to be tested, to learn Stan's results. By everyone's account, these were very unsettling encounters. Nurses and staff members who worked in fly-by-night testing facilities were known to make bets as to whether some poor, anonymous, and obviously gay man would turn up positive.

Stan and David had been soulmates for nearly twenty-three years, but a divide was opening between them. "David acts like my test was a walk in the park," Stan recalled. "Perhaps he secretly hoped that I'd be positive too, so we'd go down the path together. In a macabre way, I thought that would be fair."

After an excruciating wait, Dr. Michael Mandel—the general practitioner both Stan and David used—appeared, exchanged a few pleasantries that went right over Stan's head, and announced the test results. Stanley Rothenberg was HIV-negative.

A disbelieving Stan leaped up to see the lab report. He needed to feel the paper in his hands. "David sits quietly not saying a word," Stan later recalled. "I'd beaten the odds."

■ ■ ■

Like many HIV-infected men in those terrible years, David became an expert in his own disease, tracking his declining T-cell count the way other men follow baseball stats or the stock market. He sought out cutting-edge research, the most brilliant clinicians, and the newest treatments. Like so many, he went down the wrong paths—the immunostimulants, vitamin cocktails, ozone therapies, nostrums, panaceas, and other quackery—while applying for admittance to promising clinical trials of approved, but ultimately ineffective protocols like interleukin2 and alpha interferon.

In the beginning, Stan planned to accompany David on his quest. The furniture store was gone, but they had the resources to travel anywhere.

"We could have gone on around the world on a cruise with the money David spent on protocols that didn't work," he recalled. "But that's beside the point. When you're given a death sentence, you do whatever it takes to live another day."

But in the end, David went on his quest for a cure alone. "David was still seemingly in excellent health and does not need my assistance," Stan said, trying to explain why he stayed behind. "I felt I might end up being in the way. Perhaps he could meet another hunky HIV-positive man with whom he could have hot sex."

For Stan, the loss of the physical relationship was a profound one. It had taken him so long to come out, so long to find true love and build a life—and one cold, clinical test result had snatched all that from him. He was in mourning for what he'd lost and more than a little anxious about what was to come, compounded with profound relief and guilt that he himself had tested negative.

Amidst all those conflicting and tumultuous emotions, Stan was still deeply committed to their relationship. More than that, he knew that the loss of any physical relationship hit David just as hard as it did Stan. As healthy as David looked, as much as David believed he would find a cure, at some level they both knew the truth—David was dying. Sex, any sex, was profoundly important to both of them. In the ultimate act of love, Stan let David go alone in hopes that David might find what Stan could not provide.

Sure enough, while Stan stayed behind in Virginia, another man stepped into the picture: Jim Johnstone, whom the two met on a gay Caribbean cruise in 1987. Johnstone had family in Richmond, and he'd stayed in touch with Stan and David.

Johnstone was HIV-positive.

Johnstone's own lover had dumped him. Jim and David reconnected. They researched treatment regimens and traveled to California seeking the magic bullet.

"Jim became a surrogate lover to David, and I felt good about it." Stan insisted. "I'm no longer emotionally able to have sex with David, and Jim eases much of my guilt over all of it." He paused, then added, "People might wonder how I could get out of the picture and allow another man to love David? During the plague, untraditional things happened. Gays were already facing family rejection, religious bigotry, and discriminatory laws. After HIV hit, we were quick to organize, quick to help one another, and more open to nontraditional living arrangements. Sex for most of us was not something so monogamous and special that it could not be shared if the situation presented itself."

With David gone, Stan, sad and bored, attempted to fill

the gaping hole in his life by keeping busy. Though apprehensive, he opened a new furniture outlet, Contemporary Concepts, on Dabney Road. The 1,250-square foot store was a miniature version of Scandinavian Interiors.

"I no longer had David's know-how and creativity to lean on, so I'm forced to go it alone."

With his customer base, catalogs, a handful of reliable suppliers, and his dad providing comfort and support, Contemporary Concepts opened its doors in December 1991.

1992 passed uneventfully. Stan turned a profit. David continued to travel and research, taking his daily dose of AZT and enduring its side effects. His T4 cell count, a kind of barometer of one's ability to ward off infection, was precipitously low but seemingly holding steady.

In January 1993, Stan said, "All hell breaks loose."

David suffered bouts of uncontrollable diarrhea and his weight dropped. Immunocompromised, he was susceptible and defenseless against a number of bizarre infections and rare cancers (among them Kaposi's sarcoma, a slow-growing skin cancer that metastasizes wildly in AIDS patients). David was spared that diagnosis, but he had persistent cryptosporidiosis (crypto), a marker that carried him across the threshold from HIV-positive to AIDS.

Cryptosporidiosis is a gastrointestinal infection caused by a parasite, cryptosporidium, transmitted via water contaminated by fecal matter. Outbreaks were typical among individuals visiting water parks and public swimming pools. In most cases, the infection subsides in a few days without any intervention beyond increased fluid intake to ward off dehydration. In persons with AIDS, crypto was long-lasting, debilitating, and life-threatening. The lower a person's T4 cell count, the more likely severe symptoms and complications: prolonged diarrhea, dehydration, and ultimately, death. After treatment, the parasite will live in the intestines, dormant until awakened by further declines in a victim's immune system.

David spent February and March 1993 in and out of St. Mary's Hospital, briefly improving, then slipping further, until he came to resemble the wan, gray, ghostlike figures, victims of what equatorial Africans called "skinny disease." As the end approached, the once-vibrant, muscular, and toned man had lost more than fifty pounds, resembling in Stan's imagining, "a prisoner in a Nazi concentration camp."

On March 30, David demanded to be discharged from St. Mary's.

"He had had enough suffering and wanted to come home," Stan recalled. He remembered David gathering his few belongings and signing himself out. The pink dogwood trees, a sure harbinger of spring, were starting to bloom on Monument Avenue. On the drive home, they passed the statue of tennis star Arthur Ashe, an inadvertent AIDS victim infected by a contaminated blood transfusion.

Stan couldn't care for a dying man. David's insurance had no provision for home healthcare, and the local medical community was either unprepared or unwilling to manage end-stage AIDS patients. Stan was provided no meds, no sterile packs, no instructions on caregiving—nothing—so he arranged for a handful of volunteers to come by to assist and sit with David. Another friend, a gay physician—the frontline medics in the AIDS battle—came by each morning to give David an injection for pain. "He puts drops in his eyes to keep them lubricated," Stan recalled. "How would I know this kind of thing?"

Donnie Conner, a local psychotherapist and friend, made a point of stopping by the Monument Avenue house. "Donnie talks to David about his accomplishments in life and how much he was loved," Stan recalled. "David was concerned about what will happen to me when he dies. How brave David was! I weep uncontrollably, knowing the end was near. I try to assure him that I'd be okay, but in my heart of hearts, I really did not know."

The days ticked by, sometimes fast, sometimes agonizingly slow.

■ ■ ■

Easter Sunday. Monument Avenue shut down for the annual Easter Parade. Crowds strolled along the broad boulevard in their holiday finery, bonnets, and best suits; children in strollers were dressed as colorfully as Easter eggs. Music filled the perfumed air.

In years past, friends and neighbors gathered on Stan and David's veranda to sip wine and enjoy the festivities. "This time it was different," Stan recalled, "just another day closer to David's passing."

On the twelfth night, David found the strength to leave his bedroom. He slowly made his way down the staircase to the magnificent living room, its walls lined with Caen limestone. Again and again he tried to mouth some words to Stan, who to his despair, "blocks" him. It was the first time that had ever happened with David.

"I fail to understand," Stan remembered, "the last thing David ever spoke to me."

■ ■ ■

Friday, April 16, 1993. Stan arrived home to a silent and empty house and hurried upstairs to check on David. David's bedroom was hushed, dimly lit.

"He was breathing, but slowly, seemingly unconscious," Stan recalled. "I lie next to him, hold his limp body close. I whisper in his ear that I love him and that it was okay to let go. I repeat this over and over.

"David dies in my arms at 3:48 p.m."

■ ■ ■

Michael Coleman, a friend and former Scandinavian Interiors manager, made the arrangements with Bliley's Funeral Home to prepare David's remains for cremation. Stan couldn't bear the sight of his lover zipped into a green canvas body bag and carried outside. Stan duly fulfilled his responsibilities, inviting a handful of friends to speak at the memorial service—among them, Jim Johnstone, who'd spent many nights caring for David.

Johnstone "speaks very lovingly," Stan remembered, but his tribute ran long, touching on things Stan would have preferred left unsaid.

Stan never said a word. He told himself, "let sleeping dogs lie."

Later, it turned out that some months before David's passing, Johnstone persuaded David to finance the purchase of a condominium for him on N. W. 17th Street in Washington, DC, A very surprised Stan discovered the mortgage disbursement had come out of David's IRA account, an asset Stan inherited from David. Johnstone, whose friendship with Stan quickly faded, continued to make payments over the next few years but eventually defaulted.

Stan, who was trying to kick his benzo dependency, couldn't cope with it. It was one thing for David to sleep with a mutual friend, but it was another matter entirely to waste their community assets on what was essentially just another sex partner. It fell to Gil Rothenberg, Stan's younger brother, to sell the unit and resolve the situation.

■   ■   ■

Bad things come in threes and 1993 was no exception. In November, after David's death and Stan's discovery of the condo deal, eighty-two-year old Joe Rothenberg, recently hospitalized for cardiac problems, suffered a massive heart attack and was on life support. Stan's mother, Mollie, his younger brother, Ed, his sister Gail, and his brother-in-law, Joel, were already at the hospital.

Joseph Rothenberg had seemed to be in good health, though Stan knew he'd begun suffering mild seizures of undetermined etiology. After the typical interminable wait, an attending physician informed them that Joe's condition was irreversible.

"As a family, we agree to pull the plug and allow Dad to pass," Stan recalled. "I sat next to him, held his hand, and cried uncontrollably."

On November 3, the father, whose unwavering support and business savvy had played such a vital role in Stan's career, who'd discovered late in life the value of showing love and physical affection, and who'd embraced Stan's gay lover as a son, was gone.

"1993 was a terrible year," Stan said. "I go to work but my drive and motivation were gone."

Six months later, in the spring of 1994, Stan decided to close the Contemporary Concepts store. Six weeks later, he locked the door and turned the keys over to the landlord.

"For the rest of the 1994, I live in a daze. My friends continue to die of AIDS. My personal life was nonexistent. I turned fifty, but it feels like one hundred. I continue my daily dose of Valium, though any sense of calm was gone. I'm totally chemically dependent and live in terror of loneliness and death. I can find no reason to get off the drug. I resign myself to the rest of my life."

Sixteen

BY MID-1995, STAN was no longer willing to settle for the remnants of what he'd had before. Those odd moments when David's absence would suddenly stab him in the gut were getting further apart, and the stark loneliness and grief were fading to boredom.

Stan finally decided to take action despite his anxiety about re-entering the single scene. He placed an ad in the Personals section of *Style Weekly*, a Richmond tabloid providing alternative news and culture as well as a direct pipeline to gay and bisexual men seeking casual sexual encounters, and occasionally, more serious relationships. One of the respondents was Raymond G., a handsome thirty-something with a wife, three young children, and a major sexual identity issue.

"At the time, Ray was not yet ready to out himself," Stan recalled, "but like many such men, his feelings screamed for validation."

Ray worked an evening shift at the Federal Reserve

branch. Soon, the two were chatting on the phone and connecting for late-night quickies at Stan's house during Ray's dinner break.

"Ray was nicely built, prematurely gray, and gorgeous," Stan recalled. "To the point, I think I'm dreaming."

After the grim years of David's decline and death, Ray was outgoing, energetic, fun, and "a pianist who plays tunes by ear." The midnight encounters continued for months.

Not surprisingly, hope sprang anew in Stan's heart. With his physical needs satisfied, Stan was now open to more of life. So much of Ray reminded him of David—was it mere coincidence? Could Ray be Stan's next husband?

Reality was never completely enough and Stan's relationship with Ray was no exception. A decade later, the compelling need to live in a greater, more epic story would be Stan's undoing.

Stan believed that Ray saw him as the absolute pinnacle of gay life—open, free, and living in a historic Monument Avenue mansion. The fantasy was intoxicating enough for both men to ignore their age differences as well as the existence of Ray's wife and children.

Six months later, Ray took over David's old bedroom.

Ray, Stan recalled, brought his boys, ages ten and eight, and his daughter, four, to visit every other weekend. "We had more than enough room, plenty to eat, and they could bring over their games."

Stan, smitten with Ray, belatedly experienced all the joys and exasperations of parenting—the milk spills and wasted food at meals, the cartoons and games, the laughs, silliness, and playground bruises. "Ray's move to my home turned his family life upside-down, but he never regretted it," Stan said. "He was constantly broke but never complained. Most of his paycheck went to his wife, so I didn't put any demands on him. I didn't want money to hurt our relationship."

By Stan's account, the relationship ran smoothly and happily for nearly two years. There was never an intimation of anything untoward between Stan and the children. When the cracks in the relationship appeared, it was Ray who was the instigator.

The two worked out together at the downtown YMCA, a veritable Garden of Eden for a fallible gay man who had lived in denial and sexual frustration for most of his life. Sure enough, "Ray became friends with a man previously married with a couple of kids," Stan recalled. At the time, Stan was naively planning a first-class Australian vacation for him and Ray using frequent flyer miles.

"We're just weeks from leaving when out of the blue, Ray asks me up to his bedroom," Stan remembered bitterly. "He gives me the news that he was moving in with a man he met at the YMCA! I'm stunned. Why do these things keeping happening to me? I don't know what to think or what to do."

Once again, now fifty-three years old, Stan was alone.

1 9 9 7
Richmond, Virginia

Desperate to reconnect with the world, Stan purchased his first computer. He didn't understand much about the internet, the chat rooms, or the email, but he was determined not to be left out. He was desperate to connect with the rest of the world but was increasingly marginalized in the gay community he'd once been a poster child for.

Not only was his body beginning to betray him as he aged, but now he was alone, too, both physically and emotionally. Although he was technologically illiterate, Stan would not go gentle into that good night.

The hapless men and women working the Microsoft and AOL help desks shepherded him into the world of technology, fielding constant queries and novice questions. "I'm on a first-name basis with people in India," Stan remembered. "I was so pathetic it was comical."

Frustrated with his lack of progress and tired of deciphering foreign accents, Stan posted a personal ad looking for help.

A man named Jim Holstrom responded. A tech-savvy gay man, Holstrom lived just a few streets away. When Jim showed up, the sex Stan was hoping for didn't materialize, but Jim would become a stalwart friend and Stan's personal computer guru. With Jim's coaching and constant encouragement, Stan began to make progress. Within a few weeks, Stan had learned "just enough to be dangerous."

Holstrom was about to quit his tech job at Family Dollar, a discount retail chain. He told Stan he was moving to Fort Lauderdale, Florida, to work in a wholesale food operation run by his best childhood friend in Richmond, Dennis. The business involved purchasing overstocked foodstuffs at steep discounts and reselling to local merchants.

A few months later, Jim invited Stan, who by then had had his fill of Richmond, to move to South Florida. Scouting around, Holstrom found a two-bedroom apartment for Stan in the sprawling Oakland Park community just west of I-95.

"I'd made up my mind to sell my home and move," Stan remembered, "but downsizing from a 5,000-square foot house to a 1,500-square foot apartment was not quick or easy."

He listed his beloved Danish furnishings in *Style Weekly*, held a huge yard sale—selling $10,000 worth of David's tools for thirty cents on the dollar—left the house to a real estate agent to deal with, and flew south as the bleak winter of '97 was settling on Richmond.

In Florida, Stan embarked on a whole life makeover. His first priority was to meet people—good people. He joined a gay synagogue where he met Douglas Feldman, an anthropology professor who would remain a friend over the years.

"We went to the synagogue on many occasions," Feldman remembered. "Stan was really into it, more so than I was. He was a considerate, thoughtful, intelligent guy."

The next step was to find a psychotherapist. As Stan thumbed through the *Yellow Pages*, an advertisement caught his eye: Dr. Rick Harris, founder of the Neurofeedback Institute.

"We observe the brain in action from moment to moment," read the blurb. "We show that information back to the person and we reward the brain for changing its own activity to more appropriate pattern."

Control. Control and science. Stan liked the sound of that. He immediately made an appointment with Harris.

As with all Stan's prior therapists, Dr. Harris, a very experienced clinician, could come up with no clear-cut diagnosis or explanation for Stan's debilitating episodes of blocking. Fifteen sessions later, with scant progress made,

Harris convinced Stan to take a different approach: deal with what was now a thirty-four-year benzodiazepine dependency. Stan agreed and was referred to a rehab program run at the Sunrise Medical Center in nearby Sunrise, Florida. Nervous but hopeful, he threw a small suitcase into the car and began his journey to wellness on a warm, sunny Monday morning.

The attending physician was Dr. Richard Seely, who would later testify as a defense witness at Stan's sentencing.

After a few days at the clinic, Stan realized his anxiety and withdrawal symptoms were increasing with each decrease in benzodiazepine dosage. That made sense in the short term, but unbeknownst to him, a countdown had begun. His health insurance would only cover ten days at Sunrise. He found the Narcotics Anonymous meetings and calming therapies helpful, but always in the background, he recalled, "I see doom approaching."

Next thing he knew, he was in the hospital parking lot, discharged a few days early, left to kick the addiction on his own. Somehow, he made it to Jim Holstrom's house without driving his car off a bridge.

That Thursday night, sleepless, as waves of anxiety and panic crashed over him, Stan was convinced he was dying. The next morning, his detox, begun with such hope and optimism, was far from over. Rushing home, he ingested a dose of Valium he'd stashed away for an emergency. No relief. An hour later, he swallowed another dose. Nothing happened. *The drug no longer worked.*

A wave of sheer terror ran through his body. Thoughts of suicide became very real.

"What could I do? I just wanted my life back. Oh, G-d!"

Friday afternoon, he begged a very skeptical doctor to write a thirty-day Valium script. "I denied that I was suicidal, but I was," he remembered. "I couldn't bear to be locked away in protective custody. I just want my life back."

That lost weekend was the curtain-raiser for a three-year odyssey of isolation, loneliness, desperation, and anxiety—all consequences of his chemical dependency withdrawal. Just as David Jacks sought a magic bullet to slow the destruction of his immune system, Stanley Rothenberg wandered far afield seeking relief: naturopathic medicine, chiropractic, tai chi, yoga, juicing, acupuncture, dietary sensitivity studies, and colon cleansing, on and on.

It also marked the first time he wandered into the thoroughly addictive world of chat rooms. "I log onto AOL and go to the member-created chat room section. I know little about search engines other than AOL. I create my own chat, naming my room 'Benzos.' After an hour, a guy chimes in. We compare experiences and he offers me the first real support by legitimizing my situation and assuring me that I would 'eventually' feel better . . . (Then) a nice lady suggests massages and natural remedies such as vitamin B–12. I spend eight hours online that day and the next. I hardly eat. All I can think of was getting back on the computer and starting a chat immediately."

Instead of a cure, he had exchanged the last addiction for another.

Seventeen

FIVE YEARS AND six treatment facilities later, still grieving, Stan was searching for a way to put his life back in order. Convinced that years of benzo dependency and blocking had masked and even exacerbated his physical and psychic ills, he checked into the Austen Riggs Center in Massachusetts, a world-renowned psychiatric hospital set amidst the picturesque fields, farms, and communities that served as Norman Rockwell's inspiration. The hospital was one of six facilities where Stan was treated for debilitating anxiety, depression, blocking, and drug dependency between 1998 and 2003. Austen Riggs specialized in treatment-resistant patients—men and women "exhibiting debilitating symptoms, recurrent crises, self-destructive or suicidal behaviors, and social withdrawal." It seemed like a haven perfectly tailored for Stanley G. Rothenberg.

He spent seven months at the hospital. At the end of his stay, he still felt terribly isolated, endured the after-effects of his addiction, and was literally rendered therapeutically mute by recurrent episodes of blocking that kept him from responding to group and one-on-one therapy. There was no breakthrough.

"My in-house psychiatrist can offer no diagnosis or treatment," he recalled. "Here I am in a small town one thousand miles from home and lonely. I'm one of the oldest patients and most people simply ignore me." So many futile months at an average cost of $800 a day.

In the end, he reached out to Jim Holstrom, who flew up from Florida and accompanied Stan on the long drive home. In Richmond, they spent the night at Joel and Gail's home. Stan had a fond memory of his mother seemingly in excellent health coming by to see him there.

Twenty hours later, driving straight through, they were back in steamy Fort Lauderdale. Stan found his apartment unlivable, covered in slime and mold. Sure enough, a gay man he'd met at a Narcotics Anonymous meeting who'd promised to look after the place blew him off. As for Narcotics Anonymous, Stan would attend more than one thousand meetings during his Florida years.

"These fellow addicts were my friends," he insisted. "And I hung out with them as often as I could. I had no other friends. If anything, I thought of myself as a very sick alien touched down in Florida."

November 2002
Fort Lauderdale, Florida

One week after Stan arrived back in Florida, another vital link to his past was severed. His sister, Gail, called from

Virginia to tell him their mother was hospitalized with an upper respiratory infection that had worsened into pneumonia. By the time Stan arrived, his mother was gone.

"We kids made the joint decision to pull the plug," he remembered.

At her memorial service, Stan read a "poignant essay" he'd hastily crafted: "Mother was dedicated to her children. She wanted all of us to be successful, productive, and happy adults. She never once wavered from this. She was there for me during the most critical times of my life."

As if he sensed what lay ahead, he broke down.

In the weeks after his mother's funeral, Stan, who had applied for Social Security disability, placed a personal ad. As he recalled, "I wanted someone to work for me on weekends and to keep me company, and to drive to the food store, the beach, or a Narcotics Anonymous meeting."

Four men responded to the query, but one stood out: Ron Duron, an "affable, sociable, compassionate guy who happens to be a handsome Latino." Soon enough, Stan, benzo-free but depressed, found himself looking forward to hunky Ron's weekend visits.

2003
Fort Lauderdale, Florida

Jim Holstrom called with an offer Stan couldn't refuse: a three-bedroom beachfront condo at the Plaza East complex in Fort Lauderdale was selling well below market value. The 2,500-square foot unit, with ocean views on three sides and a wrap-around balcony, needed an extensive upgrade. Holstrom, a jack of all trades, estimated refurbishing would run an additional $50,000 and offered to handle the job.

"I wanted the unit so badly that his estimate, no matter what it was," Stan remembered, "would not have deterred me."

Stan bought the unit for $425,000 and spent the next six months happily—and this itself was a blessing—researching, and then scouring Home Depot, Lowe's, and other outlets for the right fixtures, lighting, and appliances at the right price.

"It gave me something I could do without blocking," he recalled, "something productive."

When it finally arrived, moving day was a scene right out of the *Beverly Hillbillies*. Stan and Ron Duron were caught in a cloudburst unloading furnishings from a battered pickup. In the end, he was the owner of a showcase home—totally new kitchen, marble floors, fresh paint, plastering, carpeting, track lights.

"It was gorgeous, almost breathtaking," he remembered. "The only thing missing was David, who'd grown up on the water." Stan spent another two years furnishing the condo.

Halfway through the renovations, Stan, now fifty-nine, invited Ron Duron to live with him as partners and lovers. Over the previous months, the two had grown close, but their relationship remained without a sexual component.

"I was still trying to turn my life into something productive," Stan insisted, "putting forth every ounce of energy into finding some fulfillment."

On the public service front, his attempts to volunteer

with Broward County social welfare organizations came to nothing. He was seeing another therapist, John Jamieson, on a weekly basis, still fearful of sinking back into depression "and becoming old and useless."

Duron accepted Stan's overture, but there were unspoken reservations on both sides. "I feel a love for Ron, but he was not someone with whom I can have esoteric discussions," Stan admitted. "He doesn't feel comfortable chatting about his feelings. Most men don't, but gay men generally do."

Ron, much younger than Stan, had a job—he was a UPS driver—that kept him hopping. His outside interests were active and energetic, very different from the more cerebral and inwardly-directed Stan. An ace tennis player with a shelf full of trophies, Duron spent what little free time he had refining his game; he did volunteer work, mostly for LGBT organizations. He was messy, trailing dirty clothes, dishes, magazines, and sweat socks in his wake, to the point that Stan, who had spent months furnishing and accessorizing the condo, couldn't bear to peek into Duron's untidy bedroom. A mutual friend would later describe Ron as a "forty-two-year-old kept boy."

More quickly than most, the two men slipped into familiar and often annoying routines that could steal the joy from any romantic relationship. Stan spent his mornings at Dunkin' Donuts sipping iced coffee and reading the newspapers, and his afternoons lolling at the beach, eager "to meet someone to talk to but inevitably winding up alone day after day." Too many nights, Ron arrived home from work exhausted, wolfed down the dinner Stan had carefully prepared, scanned the paper, headed for his bedroom, and fell asleep. He had to be at work very early in the morning.

Stan, with nothing but time on his hands and the limits of his passion rigidly dictated by Viagra, was increasingly frustrated. "Ron was a wonderful human being and a good friend, but he was not the person to satisfy any of my sexual needs," Stan explained. "He falls very short of what I was accustomed to in the past and desperately need now. So I spend six years trying to teach an old dog new tricks, but fail."

Among Stan's complaints, Ron never initiated sex with him. He refused to "make-out" (Stan and David were big kissers). He also declined to play "bottom" to Stan's "top." He fell asleep after he climaxed, leaving Stan fuming.

"It was work!" Stan added.

Soon enough, the blinking cursor on his computer screen became a beacon summoning him.

Clearly, the stage was being set for his downfall, but understanding Stanley Rothenberg's behavior requires peering through the lens of his all-defining sexuality. "My condo was absolutely breathtaking, but my life was not about things anymore," he explained. "More things did not equate to more happiness as I'd envisioned.

"I'm sexually unsatisfied and extremely frustrated. In my mind, it was time to try something different. It seemed the right time to let my subconscious mind take over and see where it would lead me. You can see where all this was heading—down a very slippery slope."

He met a "guy" who told him about a password-protected Russian website where "one could view anonymous postings of all kinds of images, including child porn." He stumbled on a chat room, "Fathers and Sons" or some such name. The room was so packed with users every weekend night it took some waiting to get in.

"As I scroll down the public chat content, I quickly

determine that this was a room full of users talking about incest. My curiosity was piqued. I just observe my first time there. Being someone with very loose boundaries, I find the chatter exciting and totally different from anything I'd given prior thought to. I'd just been through almost four years of pain and emotional turmoil, so I'm ripe for exploring anything that could excite me. And I do," he recalled.

"When I run across profiles of guys who sound very open-minded, I instant-message them for private chats. These chats were full of fantasy and perversions, but thoughts *were not* illegal. Some users ask me if they could use a phone and have phone sex with me."

"Why not?" Stan printed out many of these chats and stored them in his bedroom, hoping to reconnect or arrange sexual liaisons down the line.

Unbeknownst to Stan, one of the users regularly trolling the chat rooms was a hyper-aggressive Port St. Lucie detective who had busted scores of men downloading or trading child porn. His name was Neil Spector.

PART II

PUNISHMENT

Eighteen

THE DAY OF his sentencing, December 10, Stan was awakened long before dawn by two burly night shift officers. He pulled on some clothes and was escorted by elevator to the Palm Beach County Jail's basement out-processing unit. He was handed an orange jumpsuit and a pair of blue size–thirteen house slippers. The only things he was allowed to take were his reading glasses and federal identification card. The jumpsuit lacked pockets; he carried his glasses and stuffed the ID card into his sock. Ankles and wrists shackled to a chain encircling his waist, he staggered to a waiting van in the jail's adjoining parking garage. The shackles so disrupted his balance that one guard was forced to hold him steady; the other guard carried a long gun.

Stan was the only prisoner making the ninety-minute drive to the federal district courthouse in downtown Miami. It was cloudy and humid, typical South Florida weather. The van's air conditioner was blasting. He sat there shivering with cold and unease.

"How could things have gone so wrong?"

He had personally driven that slice of the I-95 corridor hundreds of times, oblivious to his surroundings, but this time he studied every billboard and mileage marker as if they bore some divine truth. Mercifully, after a while, the hum of the engine and the guards' conversation lulled him "into my own world."

At 8:30 a.m. Stan was escorted to a holding cell in the courthouse basement, quite literally a cold-steel cage. He was left there in shackles for an hour-and-a-half. Finally, a guard appeared and escorted him by elevator to the side entrance to the courtroom. No word passed between the two men.

Michael Metz and Richard Lubin were standing, talking softly at the defense table. Aside from the prosecution team, a US Marshals Service security officer, and a court reporter, the imposing courtroom was as empty as a mausoleum. At 10 a.m., District Court Judge Donald Graham swept in, accompanied by a bailiff, and majestically assumed his seat looking down at the defense table. Despite himself, Stan was reminded of the biblical story of David and Goliath "only with much less confidence of prevailing."

The first day was essentially given over to testimony by the defense's expert witnesses. Stan's witness, Dr. William Samek, built on his findings and presented a thorough, well-grounded evaluation drawn from his interviews, testing, and Stan's extensive and well-documented medical history. He assessed Stan's state of mind, his MDSO (mentally disordered sex offender) status, and the likelihood of a positive response to treatment. As for the risk of Stan committing future sex offenses against children, Samek testified that Stan "has a low risk of engaging in, or of attempting to engage in, any illegal activity with a minor ever again."

As the hours droned by, Judge Graham, realizing defense testimony and prosecution rebuttal had no likelihood of concluding in a single day, reluctantly continued the hearing. The next hearing would take place a week later, with sentencing passed at the federal courthouse in Fort Pierce. The dazed Stan was ferried back to the Palm Beach County Jail.

"I know in my mind that I've not agreed to any plea deal," Stan recalled. "I've put my full faith in Judge Graham to do the right thing. I know what kind of person I was prior to that fateful day. And I know that I'd never, ever touched a minor in my life. Given this information, wouldn't a reasonable person understand that while I used stupid judgment and behaved like an idiot, the entire crime was fictitious, and there was no victim? Wouldn't ten years be adequate punishment for a person whose life expectancy was not much more than that? I was not a pedophile and would not be a danger to society if given a second chance."

He told himself this over and over.

The hearing was reconvened in Fort Pierce the following week. None of Stan's family members show up. His lover, Ron Duron, claimed he couldn't take a day off driving his truck. His only supporter in the courtroom was an old friend, a real estate developer named Ben Alaimo.

"It was nice to see a recognizable face," Stan recalled.

A second expert witness, the addiction specialist Dr. Richard Seely (a practitioner at the Sunrise Regional Medical Center where Stan had undergone disastrous inpatient benzodiazepine detox treatment a decade earlier) testified that Stan was "grossly impaired and mentally disabled." This was the same diagnosis reached by the Social Security Administration.

However, Stan could not fail to notice that Judge Graham

seemed increasingly impatient with Seely's testimony. He declined to ask a single question of the psychiatrist. "Given the complexity of the testimony," Stan later recalled, "this seemed odd to me."

Now it was the prosecution's turn. Assistant US Attorney Rinku Talwar called Dr. Wade Meyers to the stand. Most recently a professor at Brown University's Warren Alpert Medical School and director of forensic psychiatry at Hasbro Children's Hospital in Providence, Rhode Island, Meyers was a seasoned courtroom veteran who had testified in hundreds of trials.

Meyers' stated expertise was drawn from research into "more extreme forms of violence and more extreme forms of sexual offenders." He'd barely spent two hours with Stan and administered one test. As Stan watched in horror, Meyer's testimony was not so much diagnosis, but a point-by-point repudiation of every argument and mitigating factor in his defense. With scant dissent from Judge Graham, Talwar led Dr. Meyers in a determined attempt to destroy both Stan's and his expert witnesses' credibility.

Some particularly damaging excerpts from Meyers' testimony:

Talwar: *"What actually did you observe with regard to the physical or outward appearance of Mr. Rothenberg?"*

Meyers: *"He wasn't fidgety. He didn't shift back and forth. He had no tremor in his extremities. His hands were without any sign of tremor."*

Talwar: *"Why was this significant?"*

Meyers: *"He (Rothenberg) said when I started the interview. . . that he was in some sort of severe withdrawal or terrible withdrawal. And yet, objectively, he didn't seem to be in any kind of withdrawal at all."*

Talwar: *"What symptoms would you expect to see from someone actually in withdrawal?"*

Meyers: *"Someone who was uncomfortable, that appears dysphoric (mental discomfort) or miserable emotionally. . . who should have possibly a tremor, who had trouble sitting still, perhaps some sweatiness or other signs of just general discomfort. Speech that would also show some sign of increased anxiety."*

Talwar: *"Did you observe any of these symptoms?"*

Meyers: *"His speech was of normal tone, normal rate. . . He presented as calm, rational and as a very intelligent man."*

Talwar: *"Medically speaking, was there such a thing as mental blocking?"*

Meyers: *"No."*

Talwar: *"In this (defense) report, it indicates that the defendant stated `the blocking does not occur if the topic was interesting.' What does that mean to you?"*

Meyers: *"Something that I think we're probably all guilty of. That's being human. If something was not interesting to us, our mind may wander off and find something more interesting."*

Talwar: *"Dr. Crown (another defense witness) just testified that, in his opinion, the defendant suffers from some sort of frontal lobe brain damage. Did you find any evidence that the defendant suffers from frontal lobe brain damage?"*

Meyers: *"No. . . To start with, he (Rothenberg) was a good student. He graduated from a respected college with a decent grade average. He started and ran and sustained an entrepreneurial independent furniture business. . . which would take a great deal of frontal lobe or executive functional skills to make successful. . . Look at the pictures of his house when he was arrested. There's no sign of disorganization. Its organization which reflects intact frontal lobe functioning."*

Talwar: *"These 1,200 or so pages of (seized) chats. . . the fact that they occurred over such a long period of time, what does that indicate to you in terms of whether or not this was an impulse (crime) or something else?"*

Meyers: *"You can, in a simple way break down crimes into one of two types: they can be either impulsive, i. e. emotional-based crimes, or on the other end of the spectrum, predatory crime. It was not in any way impulsive. It was carefully thought-out."*

Talwar: *"What would be the more objective examination, if you will, psychological tests after a defendant was incarcerated, or viewing his behavior before he was arrested?"*

Meyers: *"The behaviors and the writings and the pictures, those things were reality. We have them here; they were in black and white or in color. They were what was really going on. Whether test results were reality or not, who knows?"*

Talwar: *"What was your opinion as to the reliability of these tests?*

Meyers: *"They were actuarial instruments. They were not made to be applied to any given individual. They were to get a general sense."*

Talwar: *"There's been a considerable amount of the experts' reports indicating that the defendant suffers from 'generalized* *anxiety disorder.' Do you believe the defendant suffers from generalized anxiety disorder?"*

Meyers: *"In my mind, the jury was still out as to whether Mr. Rothenberg now has an anxiety disorder or not, and I'm not even sure if he had one in the past."*

Talwar: *"What about a situation in which the defendant found himself. . . meeting potentially an 11-year-old, mentally challenged child with whom to have sex. Would that be an anxiety-provoking situation?"*

Meyers: *"For the average person, it would be an extremely anxiety-provoking situation. Yet, when I spoke with Detective Spector about his impressions of how the defendant presented, he said that he came across as calm and nonchalant during the meetings in the car. . . which was not consistent with having a significant anxiety disorder."*

Talwar: *"Describe the defendant's empathy toward the potential victim?"*

Meyers: *"I asked him if he had remorse about what had happened regarding this 11-year-old, and he said he felt bad about it because he had hurt the ones he loved.*

> He made no mention of what his sexual
> acts, including intercourse, would have
> had on an 11-year-old, sexually naïve girl
> both physically and psychologically, the
> damage it would have caused."

Talwar: "Did you find the defendant to be narcissistic?

Meyers: "Yes I did. . . self-centered, a sense of entitlement, of 'I'm special,' those kinds of qualities."

Talwar: "What we all want to know here, in your opinion, was the defendant a risk for reoffending?"

Meyers: "I think he was at significant risk of committing future sex crimes. . . He said he got into the pedophilic area, the other perverse areas, due to the need for thrills, for sensation-seeking. I mean this was to give him kicks."

Dr. Meyers buttressed every aspect of the prosecution's argument. Stan said his blocking issues—the existence of which Meyers denied—prevented him from comprehending just how much damage Meyers was doing.

As Graham was readying to pronounce his sentence, Stan asked permission to address the bench. He had written a statement (he said Metz and his team never vetted it) and was granted his request.

"As I begin to speak, I break down in uncontrollable

sobs. I can't stop. I cry for at least ninety seconds. I'm trying to say that I've never touched a minor in my life, but most of what I've written was esoteric and off the wall. I mention something about a bird flying freely in the sky and make some reference to HIV too. What I said was weird, really."

He didn't do himself any good. No mercy or mitigation was forthcoming from the bench.

On Count One, Judge Graham ordered Stan to federal prison for 300 months (twenty-five years). If he survived, he would be eighty-seven years old at his release. But there was more: prison was to be followed by supervised release for the remainder of his life. On top of all this, Graham imposed a $25,000 fine and a ten-year sentence on Count Two, which he ordered to run concurrently.

"Graham began by expressing visible anger that not only had I solicited a young girl, but that she was also handicapped!" Stan remembered. "What? She was handicapped? What was he talking about? A real handicapped girl? Given this preface, I knew the sky would fall. And it did."

He said Michael Metz fled the courtroom without uttering a word. Lubin came over and apologized. Another spectator in the courtroom that day recalled Stan was so flummoxed and confused that he seemed unaware of how long 300 months was.

As he was led out in shackles, the bailiff whispered, "Twenty-five years."

■ ■ ■

That afternoon, he was shipped back to Palm Beach County Jail. "I'm not in shock," Stan recalled, "I'm stupefied. It was all too surreal to comprehend. None of the other inmates can believe it either. All they can say was that my sentence will surely be amended on appeal. I don't know how. I have no knowledge of the appeals process."

The following morning, the corrections officer in charge of Stan's unit told him he had a visitor.

"I'm 100-percent sure it had to be Michael Metz," Stan recalled. "I'm foaming at the mouth in anticipation."

He was led to a small secure room where legal visits were conducted. In walked Jonathan Kaplan, one of Metz's associates. Stan stood there agog. "How can Metz send a representative after what just happened to me! Didn't he have enough courage to show up in person?

"The first thing out of Kaplan's mouth was Metz wanted to appeal this egregious sentence and he knows exactly how to do it! I tell him I need to think everything over. The truth was it was not likely that I would hire Lubin & Metz ever again! Kaplan tells me 'the clock was ticking' and leaves.

"I'm a ball of anger and confusion."

■ ■ ■

Stan was transferred to the high-rise Federal Detention Center (FDC) in Miami for processing and classification (getting designated) to a federal prison where he would begin serving his sentence. He was hoping for Federal Correctional Institute (FCI) Petersburg, a medium-security prison an hour's drive from Richmond. He spent four months in Miami, a big step up from the "inhumane warehouses of evil," he called the county jails.

"No medical or dental treatment, no psychological care.

The food was something you wouldn't consider giving to your family dog."

At the time, he was medically stable thanks to the two mg Klonopin he was been taking. That first week in Miami, he met with the facility's staff psychiatrist and poured out his story.

"I implore her to allow me to continue my Klonopin," he remembered.

"What was your outdate (discharge)?" she asked.

"After a long pause, I answer '2030.' I know at that moment my chances of staying on a benzo were zero."

He insisted that she call a higher-up at the Bureau of Prisons (BOP) officials in Washington. She "reluctantly agrees to make the call." Stan was immediately turned down and sent back to his ninth-floor pod. He was allowed a gradual reduction in dosage for ten days (he'll never be prescribed benzodiazepine again), and that was it. Soon enough, he was enduring yet another debilitating benzo withdrawal.

"In all my years of incarceration," he recalled, "my time at FDC Miami was the worst period of all. The stress of putting together an appeal, the twenty-five-year sentence, and everything else became too much to bear. I'm close to full meltdown." He spent four months in this precarious state on the knife edge between life and death and caring little about either.

Nineteen

2009
Federal Correction Institute
Petersburg, Hopewell, Virginia

ON APRIL 28, Stan arrived in Virginia after a grueling twelve-hour ride in a converted old Greyhound bus, shackled and handcuffed the whole way. The trip was an ironic parallel to the journey he and David had taken so many years before when they began their lives together, a fact not lost on Stan. For lunch, he was handed a baloney sandwich, potato chips, an apple, and four cookies.

"Getting up from my seat and walking to the toilet at the rear of the bus while the bus was doing seventy-five mph was an acrobatic activity," he recalled. Wriggling out of his orange jumpsuit to relieve himself was an even bigger challenge that he ignominiously failed.

He was trying to process all the wretched twists and turns a life could possibly take as he stared at the four somber concrete slabs and enclosed grass compound that make up FCI Petersburg located in Hopewell, Virginia, near the confluence of the James and Appomattox rivers.

In the distance Stan heard motor boats plying the river and occasionally the mournful wail of a freight train.

"I live," he recalled, "in a very different solar system."

Behind its vaguely colonial facade and carefully pruned hedges was a depressing warren of cellblocks, administrative buildings, commissary, law library, and recreation area, home to approximately 2,800 convicts, all wrapped up in the unloving embrace of razor wire.

Aside from the occasional celebrity inmate—former Newark, New Jersey, mayor Sharpe James served eighteen months here for a fraud conviction—FCI Petersburg was notable for a population of notorious sex offenders. Among them, Eric Toth (twenty-five years), a child pornographer and "Ten Most Wanted" fugitive apprehended after fleeing to Nicaragua; Roger Loughry Sr. (thirty years), administrator of the *Cache,* an online bulletin board where more than one thousand members from around the world shared child porn; Richard Chandler (twenty-five years), a former Tennessee police officer convicted in the largest child pornography prosecution in US history; Rabbi David Kaye (six years), an internet predator convicted of coercion and intent to engage in illicit sexual conduct with a thirteen-year-old boy. Kaye was notorious enough to have been featured on the NBC series, *To Catch a Predator*.

In this company, Stan was small fry. Nonetheless, he was facing as much or more prison time than many men convicted of multiple grievous offenses against flesh-and-blood children. Some of these individuals, who clearly remained menaces to society, were due to be released long before Stan.

Like the dutiful schoolboy he was, Stan studied the pages of rules and regulations in his BOP handbook. He

wrote down the name and title of every corrections officer and staff member he encountered, took notes on each
conversation, and made lists of daily activities, schedules,
and events, as if prison were a test he needed to pass.

"My life was now owned and operated by an all-pow-
erful force—the Federal Bureau of Prisons," he said, "and
there would be severe punishment for not following the
pages and pages of rules and regulations found in the BOP
handbook given to each arrival at orientation. I had never
served in the armed forces and knew nothing about the
ranking system employed and the layers of responsibility.
Who were these people?"

Assigned to housing unit E-South, he quickly learned
how consciously and determinedly segregated the world
was behind bars—by race, by crime, by sexual orientation,
by ethnicity. Not surprisingly, he gravitated toward gay
sex offenders, all of whom turn out to be Caucasian.

"The first question out of my mouth after meeting a gay
sex offender is," Stan recalled, "'How much time did you
get?' I was obsessed with comparing sentences. The one
common thread I'd discover among all sex offenders was
over-sentencing. For most of us it was our first brush with
the law and none of us was guilty of any hands-on behavior. Yet, we're removed from society for five, ten, fifteen or
more years?"

His appeal was at the top of his mind, floating seemingly just out of reach, a life preserver in a turbulent sea.
"I clung to the hope," he said, "that someone would come
to their senses and determine that my sentence was cruel."

After stumbling through the fog and pain of another
benzo withdrawal, Stan found his way to the prison's
law library. Soon, he was unleashing torrents of letters
to family, friends, the ACLU, the Sentencing Project (a

prisoners' advocacy group), his US congressman, and Virginia senators Jim Webb, Mark Warner, and Tim Kaine. Only Webb responded with more than a cursory note, and he followed up with a letter to Warden Patricia Stansbury querying her about Stan's medical care. Most officials didn't bother to reply at all.

Before leaving FDC Miami, Stan had come across a San Francisco-based attorney named Alan Ellis. He recalled, "All I know was he was Jewish and had written a book on incarceration." In fact, Alan Ellis was a past president of the National Association of Criminal Defense Lawyers and a Fulbright Scholar. He reached out to Ellis.

In February 2009, at Stan's request, Michael Metz officially notified the court he was no longer Stan Rothenberg's attorney of record, ending what had become a very strained relationship. Among other complaints, Stan believed Metz and his team should have used his internet addiction/fantasy life to buttress his defense. He hoped to use that angle in his appeal. In any event, a ruling by the Eleventh Circuit Court of Appeals in Atlanta was a long shot.

The only good news was that FCI Petersburg was less than an hour's drive from Richmond. Stan's sister and brother-in-law, Gail and Joel Lewis, and many of his old friends and associates were still there. His parents were deceased, his three brothers scattered and busy with careers, families, and traumas of their own. Gail had not seen her big brother since his arrest almost a year earlier.

"In the beginning," she recalled, "it was horrific just trying to process everything that was going on. Stan was in Port St. Lucie, and he was a mess. I thought, 'I don't need to get involved in this thing. I don't know what to say or do. Gil and Doug, my brothers, were discussing things with him. I'm just a spectator.' The whole mess was... icky."

Gail wondered if the desperate and distraught man she was visiting in prison could possibly be the same Stan she jitterbugged with as a teen, the incessant scribbler and note-taker busy with his books, the lonely sixteen-year-old stung by a high school fraternity's blackball, the neighborhood activist agitating over a dearth of parking spaces, the Human Relations Commission member, speaking out for an oppressed minority? Soon, she realized the broken man before her eyes was still all those things, and she still loved and cared for him. Stanley Rothenberg was all those people, but he was also subsumed into society's most toxic label—a convicted child sex offender and felon.

■ ■ ■

A federal prison was about as far removed from Gail and Joel Lewis's real life as Mongolia. They run a promotional products company; previously, Joel owned a debt purchasing company. Neither had any concept of the world that had swallowed up Stanley, the myriad rules and regulations, the petty tyrants and arbitrary decisions that, in the end, made everyone feel like a criminal.

"You go through processing like you go through airport security," Joel recalled. "Once you pass all that, a person walks you over to an airlock and he stamps you with an ultraviolet stamp. Then you walk three feet and it's read. The person who reads it was the same person who put the stamp on.

"When you finish (visiting), that same person brings you back. He puts the ultraviolet light on and said, 'You're not stamped.' And he was serious. Now you're subject to whatever disciplinary action he chooses to impose. 'Wait a minute,' I want to scream, 'You stamped me! I went with you! You're bringing me back and telling me I don't have the stamp you gave me?'

"And he said, 'It was not there.'

"And I think, 'Oh crap. How am I going to fight this one?'

"And he looks at me and said, 'Well okay, I'll let it go this time. Don't let it happen again.'

"This time!"

"If you argue, they make a note in a book. So it was 'I'm sorry. I made the mistake.' It was extremely stressful to be there."

Gail was flagged when her bra and shoes didn't pass muster. Sometimes, the visiting hours and days were switched without notice, and an hour's drive to visit came to naught.

"What I keep saying is," Gail insisted, "Thank God we're on the other side.'"

Stan was on the inside where things were much worse.

■ ■ ■

FCI Petersburg is one of ten federal prisons offering sex offender management programs (SOMP) created to handle a growing population of such inmates—nearly 12,000 out of a total federal prison population of 210,000 in 2015. The vast majority were men; an increasing number have been convicted of possession, receipt, or distribution of child pornography. Branded pedophiles, perverts, chicken hawks, and worse, these inmates were themselves at-risk populations within a prison's walls, targets of the normal run of murderers, thieves, armed robbers, neo-Nazis, violent gangbangers, and other felons.

"They tend to be harassed, attacked, and brutalized,"

wrote Christopher Zoukis, a prison rights activist and inmate who oversees the *Prison Law* blog, a resource for inmates, families, attorneys, and criminal justice professionals. "This was part of institutional culture, if not supported by the prison administration then accepted by it as inevitable. In many penal institutions, once identified, *chomos* (inmate slang for child molester) were forced to reside in Special Housing Units (solitary confinement) for their own protection. If not, they were likely to be 'beat off' the yard by a mob of violent thugs who assault them—often in sight of prison guards happy to look the other way." To be homosexual and a convicted *chomo*—Stanley Rothenberg— is roughly like being in the seventh circle of hell.

At Petersburg, he underwent additional rounds of assessment, evaluation, and monitoring. In theory at least, such testing helped to determine whether a sex offender was likely to engage in further risk-relevant behavior. In the gritty reality of the prison yard, it was almost laughable. Sexual violence, manipulation, and intimidation have been endemic in penal institutions for centuries.

As time passed, Stan's abject fear and uncertainty faded into the repetitive boredom of prison life. Stan began to settle in and make friends.

"The gay community at FCI Petersburg stuck together for the most part," he recalled. "That was very important to me. In my mid–60s, I was an old man. Gay men learn very early that our appearance means everything, and men of my era were always on the prowl. I was very successful at it, so it became part and parcel of who I am. Being old in a closed society like a prison meant I suddenly was very ugly and of no value to most inmates. The young, gay inmates, however, accepted me as I was, defects and all. That was a relief.

"Also, for the first time in my life," he continued, "I got to know people who either wanted to get a sex change or were already at the first stage, receiving female hormones prior to surgery. These were beautiful human beings who simply need some plumbing work to be who they really are. They've suffered enough."

To pass the endless hours, Stan became a dedicated Scrabble player. His community activist genes kicked back in, and he started evaluating the food served at the prison and presented his findings in good faith ("I believe in the power of feedback.") to the institution's Food Service Administrator. Stan believes he effected some small change for the good of the inmates.

"At one point," he recalled, "a small group of us gays start going to a weed-infested area of the rec (recreation) yard during nice weather," he said. "We bring along sunscreen, some snacks, and towels to lie down on . . . and pretend we're at the ocean. We nickname the area Peter Beach.

Eventually, the prison administration got wind of what were essentially innocent goings-on and declared the beach out of bounds."

With a college education and vulnerable aura, Stan was also quick to be victimized. Again, his hunger for romance proved his undoing.

"I'm a very needy inmate who needs personal attention," he recalled. "I'm serving a life sentence. I've lost my condo and all my worldly possessions. I own nothing. I'm not having sex. With ED (erectile dysfunction), I can't even jerk off! What's the point of going on living? I ask myself this question every day for months.

"One afternoon while typing in the law library, I overhear an inmate explaining a legal issue to the man sitting next to him. I introduce myself. The young guy lives in the same housing unit as I do. To someone unfamiliar with the legal system, he appears to know quite a bit. I'm still in benzo withdrawal and blocking to the point where I'm not able to comprehend any legal stuff. I feel powerless over my future. Soon, I find myself comfortable leaning on him for legal advice. He shows me attention and gives me hope. I latch onto him like an orphan in a strange land.

"Whenever he researches a legal question for me, I pay him with commissary items, something most inmates use to expunge debts. As it turns out, he was in prison for murder. I don't remember details of the crime, but he was apparently under eighteen, and was tried and sentenced as an adult. This happened in Washington, DC, and drugs were involved.

"We were good friends, that's all. He even gives me his mother's phone number so I can speak to her and let her know how her son was faring. He had had some tragic breaks in his life, and I feel sorry for him. In my second year in Petersburg, our friendship morphs into a closer relationship. I stock up his locker. In my mind, but only in my mind and not in reality, he was my lover. I want to hold hands and walk with my arm around his shoulder, both, of course, taboo behaviors. I'm that naïve . . ."

In 2010, he "confides" in Stan. He said he was being visited by an FBI agent to whom he was providing information that will be used to solve a crime. He said that as a Confidential Informant (CI), he was eligible to file a 5K1.-1 motion for early release. (N. B. Section 5K.-1 of the Sentencing Guidelines under which a convict's prison sentence may be reduced by providing "substantial assistance" during a criminal investigation.)

"He said he can get me included as a CI," Stan recalled.

"I'd have to take the stand and testify at a trial. Afterward, I, too, could file a 5K1.-1. motion. He tells me it will cost $5,000 to set up the deal."

As that point, the story got more convoluted. The defendant in the case he was working on was an innocent man entrapped by the "Feds."

"He swears this was real and ongoing. He tells me being granted CI status was the only way I'll ever be released from federal custody. Blinded, I force Joel Lewis (his brother-in-law who holds power of attorney) to deposit $5,000 into this man's prison account."

After much argument and furious resistance, Joel deposits the money.

"As I wait to hear from the FBI, this friend involves himself in my case," Stan said. "He offers—for a fee—to write a 2225 to submit to the courts (18 US Code Section 2255—a motion to vacate, set aside, or correct a sentence)." In the motion, Stan argues ineffective assistance of counsel as grounds for a reversal or retrial.

"The price was well under $1,000," Stan continued. "He researches my case and shows me legal data to support his work. It all looks and sounds completely legit—it was legitimate—it was poorly done. I don't know any better."

Meanwhile, the confidential informant scheme rolled along. "He even gives me the name and phone number of his FBI contact and encourages me to phone him. I don't because I'm afraid I'll say the wrong thing and sabotage the entire plan. Time passes.

"One day, an inmate pulls me aside and said he was seen walking the track with a new admirer. This guy was claiming to be his boyfriend. My supposed friend was getting commissary from him too. Of course, I refuse to believe any of it."

Of course it was true. The "friend" was a cheap hustler and con artist, not only a familiar figure in every jail but also in every cheesy law and order series on TV. The confidential informant hustle was a scam only someone as trusting and naïve as Stanley Rothenberg would possibly fall for. Ironically, this was the same man the courts decided was a cold and calculating predator who should never see the light of day again.

"With very little notice," Stan continued, "the Bureau of Prisons orders me to pack my property for a transfer to FCI Seagoville (Low), a minimum-security penitentiary transfer center outside Dallas, Texas. It hits me that my Richmond family and friends will no longer be able to visit me. This was all too much! A terrible sense of doom, of loss and separation overwhelms me. Suddenly, all his lies and betrayal were not very important."

Once a predator gets his claws into a victim, it doesn't let go. Stan arrived at FCI Seagoville on February 24, 2011. He was still trying to adjust to life at the minimum security facility when a letter bearing a postmark and return address of the US District Court for the Eastern District of Virginia arrived in the mail. The thought briefly crossed his mind that the government realized it had made a tragic mistake in prosecuting him and relief was in the works. Tearing open the letter, he discovered that his friend was now suing him for breach of contract. According to the complaint, Stan owed him thousands of dollars for his "legal work." He was demanding punitive damages. Included in the documentation, Stan recalled, were forged legal documents and contracts.

The friend had filed his lawsuit pro se (on his own behalf). Not surprisingly, the prison system is a breeding ground for pro se cases. Convicts demand relief from everything from unjust convictions to the thickness of their mattresses. They have become a plague on the judicial system, but every judge was sworn to take them seriously. In prison, a convict loses many but not all constitutional rights. Jailhouse lawyers know this and constantly work the system looking for an out. The lawsuit would be time-consuming and costly to counter.

"Now what do I do?" Stan groaned.

Brother-in-law Joel Lewis stood by Stan long after his lover, Ron Duron, and Stan's own brothers backed away. As cautious and prudent as Stan was reckless and naïve, Joel believed completely in the righteousness of the government and judicial system. He also had come to believe that same system had tragically over-sentenced Stanley Rothenberg to the point of cruel and inhumane punishment. Joel was stubborn. He would do everything in his power to undo the wrong and save Stan from his own naiveté.

Joel retained a well-respected Richmond attorney, Russell R. Johnson III, to defend Stan. Six months and numerous depositions and appearances later, the district court finally threw out the other inmate's lawsuit.

"It was a shakedown," Joel said. "We found that he had sued numerous other inmates. His suit against Stan was bogus on two fronts. First, he was not an attorney and could not give legal advice. Second, under Bureau of Prison rules, inmates were barred from charging for any kind of advice. When we brought this to the attention of the BOP, they simply ignored us. We had to win in court at the district level. We do and then the SOB appeals the case! By the time we get through the appeals process, it wound up costing Stan another $23,000."

How could the man who the prosecutors swore was a cold, calculating predator be taken in so easily?

PART III

APPEAL

Twenty

June 2010
Eleventh Circuit Court, Atlanta, Georgia

STAN'S HOPE THAT his "open plea" would move District Judge Donald Graham to leniency proved another mad fantasy. Sentenced to two-and-half decades in federal prison, Stan's next step was to file an appeal.

In simplest terms, there are two ways to overturn a federal criminal conviction: direct appeal and habeas corpus.

A direct appeal is lodged with the circuit court overseeing the district where the prosecution was held (in Stan's case, the United States Court of Appeals, Eleventh Circuit, which had jurisdiction over appeals from Alabama, Florida, and Georgia). If that didn't work, the next step was the US Supreme Court.

There was no question that Stan would appeal his sentence. Both he and his family were convinced that what was essentially a life sentence for talking dirty on the internet was unjust, unfair, and unreasonable.

Stan no longer trusted any of his attorneys, so the search started for a post-conviction attorney.

In Miami, Stan met a prisoner named Flowers and asked him if he knew any good appellate lawyers. Flowers recommended Linda Sheffield, an experienced appellate attorney with an excellent track record. Sheffield, based in Atlanta, had represented several sex offenders.

After interviewing Sheffield and a few other attorneys, Joel Lewis was leaning toward retaining Sheffield. "Linda was far and away above the rest," Lewis recalled.

Stan, however, decided to go with Alan Ellis in San Francisco whom he'd somehow discovered was a "very in-demand lawyer." (Later, Stan would say he can't remember how exactly Ellis's name came to him, other than the fact the lawyer had "written a book about incarceration.") On Stan's instruction, Joel Lewis dutifully wrote Alan Ellis a check for $50,000.

Ellis did indeed prove to be very much in demand. Stan was soon complaining that his secretary literally refused Stan's phone calls unless he had scheduled a pre-arranged appointment—no easy trick from prison.

"It took about forty-five days for Ellis to review all the documents," Stan recalled. "I spoke with him, and he basically gives me assurances that he understands my legal issues and would base my appeal on two of the many enhancements applied to my case."

Ellis assigned Yale Law grad Peter Goldberger, who lived in Ardmore, Pennsylvania, near Philadelphia, to research and write the appeal. "It turns out Goldberger was Ellis's right-hand man," Stan said. In fact, Goldberger's expertise was post-conviction federal criminal cases, sentencing, and Supreme Court petitions, seemingly a good fit. Six months later, the appeal was done.

This was standard practice, except that Stan, who already felt ill-used by his first round of attorneys, claimed he'd never heard of Goldberger until after the appeal was filed.

"Alan Ellis assured me he'd reviewed Goldberger's work before filing with the circuit court," Stan said, "but I felt sort of duped. Alan should have told me he'd have someone else working on my appeal. But at that point it was water over the dam, and I did not belabor it."

When the Eleventh Circuit notified Ellis and Goldberger they would hear oral arguments in the case, Stan dared to hope. "A good sign," he said, "since oral arguments were not requested unless the Court sees some merit in a case. Peter seems very professional and v ery capable. He was given fifteen minutes to make my case and the government had fifteen minutes to rebut. I phone Peter at the conclusion of his appearance and he tells me he felt good about how it went. And I begin to feel good."

At Stan's December 2008 sentencing hearing, Judge Donald Graham had accepted every prosecution argument, found that the enhancements were present, and added the time for the enhancements to Stan's base sentence. He did allow a two-year reduction from the report's recommended twenty-seven-year sentence because of the defendant's mental health issues, which meant Stan would be eighty-seven rather than eighty-nine years old upon his release.

The first prong of Ellis' strategy on appeal was to attack the "pattern of activity" Guidelines enhancements. Those added ten to twelve years to Stan's sentence, which put him away for twenty-five years.

At sentencing, prosecutor Rinku Talwar had relied on transcripts of two instant message conversations between Stan and an adult male to prove up the enhancements.

The conversations took place on December 21, 2006, and Friday, June 1, 2007.

Printouts of both conversations were seized along with hundreds of other printouts of chat room exchanges in his condominium. In both, Talwar argued, Stan "actively coached and encouraged the other adults in graphic detail about how to sexually abuse minors in their care or under their influence."

In one sense, this was true. It's as true as surly teen-ager screaming, "I hate you, I wish you were dead!" to a parent. It's as true as a teenage boy ogling centerfolds with his buddies and bragging about his sexual prowess. The words form complete and coherent thoughts, but the reason that they're spoken has little to do with their actual content. They're expressions, overstated, of emotions and desires that bear little resemblance to reality.

It's in that context that the two chats—two out of boxes and boxes of printouts—should be evaluated. These con-versations, as unsettling as they are, are word porn rather than actual statements of intentions to commit crimes.

What was never adequately evaluated by Stan's defense team *before his plea* was whether Stan's damning words represent actual intent or just raw sexual fantasizing. And once Stan pleaded guilty, all questions of intent to commit the crime were irrelevant, at least as it related to the charges.

But those two conversations play a second role in the sentencing. The AUSA offered them to prove a pattern of behavior, as an enhancement on the sentence, and the courts are split on whether factors in enhancement must be proved beyond a reasonable doubt.

Stan pleaded guilty to the charges, so the govern-ment was not obligated to prove the element of intent as it relates to the actual charge. But what was at issue was his intent during the chats that were admitted to support the enhancement. Did he intend to advocate child abuse? Or was he essentially just talking dirty on the internet?

Did this openly-gay community activist with no history of interest in women or children intend to convince others in the chat to have sex with children? Or were the chats just voyeuristic fantasies?

In the years after Stan's conviction, courts struggling to determine intent have become increasingly willing to listen to testimony on pornography and internet addictions.

On appeal, Attorney Goldberger argued that neither of these chats "without more," rose to the level of a substantial step toward the commission of a crime. "(Therefore) it followed that neither of the chats can be considered as a part of any pattern of illegal conduct triggering application the Sentencing Commission enhancements."

Goldberg continued, "[M]ere talk or speech unaccompanied by some other form of overt conduct cannot constitute a substantial step necessary to an attempt to commit an offense." And if "speech alone can amount to an attempt," he asserted, "the talk or speech involved in this case was factually insufficient to rise to that level."

The second issue Stan hoped to raise in his appeal was the degree to which his well-documented benzodiazepine addiction, mental instability, and depression—he checked *himself* into psychiatric hospitals five times in the years prior to his crime—fueled his behavior. That mental illness, Stan felt, showed that he was acting based on mental illness rather than from an intent to harm a child, and that evidence of mental illness should have been a factor in mitigation.

By all accounts, both arguments were well-reasoned, fact-based, and delivered persuasively at oral argument.

■ ■ ■

Months later, two Eleventh Circuit judges, Stanley F. Birch and Stanley Marcus, along with a visiting district judge, William Terrell Hodges (serving by designation), unanimously rejected Stan's appeal. As excerpted:

"To establish an attempt as a crime, proof was required that the defendant intended to commit the underlying criminal offense with the requisite mens rea (state of mind) and that the defendant engaged in conduct which constituted a substantial step toward the commission of that crime and which strongly corroborates the defendant's criminal intent.

"The absence of a real minor victim was meaningless because the essence of the crime was the attempted enticement of someone the defendant believes to be a minor, not actual engagement in sexual activity with a minor.

"Proof was not required that the defendant must have communicated directly with a minor, either real or fictitious; dealing with an adult intermediary for the purpose of attempting to entice a minor into sexual activity with the defendant or some third person was sufficient to constitute the offense.

"That leaves, therefore, the question presented here as to whether a sexually solicitous communication by means of interstate commerce, without more, can ever constitute a substantial step toward commission of an offense in violation of 18 USC. § 2422(b)."

The judges cited a number of precedents involving sexually explicit chat room conversations with or about fictitious minor children. In one failed appeal, the court said, "The defendant's predatory designs never went beyond the chat room conversation. Yet, viewing the totality, the defendant had crossed the line from mere talk to inducement."

Stan had gone further, making that fateful journey to meet undercover Detective Neil Spector in Port St. Lucie where he was arrested.

In the end, the court said:

"We reach the same conclusion in this case. Our aim was not to decide whether [the defendant's] conduct was at least as 'criminal' as the conduct of others convicted (defendants) . . . Each of our precedents holds no more than that a reasonable jury could have found . . . None guesses at, or purports to have identified the minimum conduct that section 2422(b) (coercion and enticement of minors) proscribes.

"Stan's chats were specific instructions to adults with influence over young children; these graphic guides to sexual exploitation showed the adults both how, physically, to molest the children and how, emotionally, to persuade the children to comply with the abuse . . .

"We discern no clear error in the district court's finding that Rothenberg's chats crossed the line between sexual banter and criminal persuasion, inducement or enticement, and that he engaged in a *pattern of activity* involving prohibited sexual conduct justifying application of the enhancements provided for . . . We further conclude that the sentence was both procedurally and substantively reasonable.

"Affirmed."

"Denied?" Stan asked in disbelief when he learned of the court's decision. "Turned down on both enhancements with a 3–0 vote!"

He didn't even bother to read the ruling when Goldberger mailed it to him. "I'm so full of depression and anxiety, he recalled, "but I'm careful not to share my condition with the prison staff. They'd throw me in the hole on suicide watch. That's the last thing I need. "

Years later, he returned to that defining moment. "Finally, I understand why the Eleventh Circuit was considered the most conservative of all thirteen US circuit courts. It was another piece of the puzzle that had convinced me and so many others that the entire criminal justice system was rigged. It really was rigged against all defendants, and especially the disadvantaged and the poor," he said.

This point is amply proved by the sentencing matrix attached as an appendix. Well-connected or celebrity abusers consistently walk out with minimal sentences, while people like Stan receive maximum penalties.

Twenty-one

"It was unlikely that Mr. Rothenberg would have actually performed a sex act with a child. He was not a pedophile and does not derive primary sexual attraction from children."

—Dr. David N. Greenfield

2011
Collateral Attack

AFTER A DIRECT appeal fails, defendants are left with what are called collateral attacks. The first of these is normally a petition for a writ of habeas corpus, which is filed with the trial court, often referred to as the "court of first instance."

Literally, habeas corpus means "produce the body." But the body referred to is not the actual physical body, which would be a direct attack on the evidence. In this context, the writ requests the court to order an official to appear so the court can determine if the detention is lawful.

Most people are familiar with the term in the context

of criminal defense attorneys seeking to delay the imposition of the death penalty. In those cases, the writ is asking the court to find the order to execute is unlawful.

If granted, a writ of habeas corpus opens the door for a collateral attack on the evidence, testimony, procedure, etc. used in the original trial to win a conviction. With antecedents running all the way back to English Common Law, the Supreme Court has acknowledged the writ "as the fundamental instrument for safeguarding individual freedom against arbitrary and lawless state action. (It must be) administered with the initiative and flexibility essential to ensure that miscarriages of justice were surfaced and corrected." In 1830, Chief Justice John Marshall wrote that the "great object" of habeas corpus "is the liberation of those who may be imprisoned without sufficient cause."

In Stan's case, the writ was "seeking redress of an injustice," the injustice being the sentence and enhancements. Unfortunately for Stan, his court of first instance was the US District Court, Southern District of Florida where his nemesis, Judge Donald Graham, presided.

Stan had no doubt that his sentence fell within the scope of "imprisoned without sufficient cause." It was still simply inconceivable that he was going to spend the rest of his life in prison for talking dirty on the internet.

Unsatisfied with the work of his attorney on his direct appeal, Stan turned to Atlanta post-conviction attorney Linda Sheffield, the very same lawyer he'd overlooked during his direct appeal. "As I recall, Sheffield was first recommended to me by an inmate named Flowers I met in FDC Miami," Stan said. "I knew she'd handled federal 2255 motions (ineffective assistance of counsel), and this time I made sure to telephone her. We had a nice chat, and I was impressed with the way she answered my questions. I decided to forego additional interviewing and hired Linda.

"Linda was now my fifth hire to represent me, and I was yet to get any victory anywhere. At this point I've spent more than $300,000 and I'm still sitting in prison with a twenty-five-year sentence hanging over me."

A habeas corpus writ gives the court broad discretion in fashioning relief for an imprisoned petitioner. The court can dismiss the charges, order a retrial, or resentence the petitioner.

The other major difference between a direct appeal and a writ is that a direct appeal is decided on the record of trial. A writ, however, can give a defendant the right to present new evidence. The habeas writ (28 USC. § 2255) typically alleges a violation of a defendant's Sixth Amendment right to effective counsel.

Now on his fifth attorney, Stan was convinced that's exactly what his problem has been. There was no other explanation for the fact that he was where he was.

Technically, Sheffield's plan was to mount a collateral attack, showing that errors in procedures or evidence were resulting in an unjust detention, i.e., sentence. Then she would ask the court to use its broad discretion to overturn Rothenberg's conviction or reduce his sentence.

"You mount a 2255 attack," said Sheffield, "when, for example, a defense lawyer doesn't raise certain issues, doesn't do an investigation, doesn't call witnesses who could have explained the case to the client's benefit."

In the best of worlds, Judge Graham would grant the habeas motion, review the new evidence and arguments that Sheffield presented, and rule to vacate Rothenberg's conviction or reduce his prison time dramatically. "Our biggest challenge was trying to show that Stan was drawn to the internet because he was mentally ill," Sheffield said. "It wasn't real. Stan never really believed that someone was going to have sex with their own child!"

■ ■ ■

In the first decade of the twenty-first century, when Stanley Rothenberg stumbled into the secret, perverse, and amoral world of internet chat rooms, the notion of an internet addiction as a profound and debilitating pathological process was practically unheard of. Today, the disorder is widely accepted and well-defined, with research suggesting that 70 percent of internet addicts—Stan included—suffer from other addictions, including drugs and sex. Such individuals use the fantasy world of the internet to escape the unpleasant feelings and stressful situations existing in their daily lives.

Dr. Beverly Young, founder of the Center for Internet Addiction, a pioneering diagnostic and treatment facility in Bradford, Pennsylvania, defined internet addiction as "any online-related, compulsive behavior which interferes with normal living and causes severe stress on family, friends, and loved ones . . . Behavior that completely dominates the addict's life . . . including a preoccupation with being online, lying, or hiding the extent or nature of the online behavior, and an inability to control or curb that behavior. When they have taken control of addicts' lives, these compulsions were unmanageable.

"Like food or drugs in other addictions," Young continued, "the internet provides the high and addicts become dependent on this cyberspace high to feel normal. They substitute unhealthy relationships for healthy ones. The loss of self-esteem grows, fueling the need to escape even further into addictive behaviors."

Young's definition could have been written from Stan's life: the irrational behaviors, the sexting and compulsive printing out of chat room exchanges, his concealing his surreptitious internet surfing from his lover Ron Duron, and close friends like Doug Feldman and Ben Alaimo, the laptop computer he felt compelled to literally hide under his bed, the recklessness—driving a hundred miles to Port St. Lucie to visit a potential cyber lover made flesh. To round out the portrait, internet addicts like Stan typically suffer from depression, mood disorders, social disorders, and anxiety disorders.

To Linda Sheffield's surprise, very little of this mitigating evidence had been developed or presented by Stan's trial defense attorneys, Metz and Lubin. "Yes, it was the beginning of all this internet stuff," she said in 2015. "A defense was still being developed, but there were people out there who could help you, who had the ability to take things further, but you had to go the extra mile."

She paused, then added, "There were lawyers who just go through the motions and do certain things and hire the usual experts. Stan's attorneys did the job, but didn't really do the job."

To do the job, Sheffield engaged Dr. David N. Greenfield, a noted psychologist and director of the Center for Internet and Technology Addiction in West Hartford, Connecticut. (Greenfield's institution was independent of Beverly Young's Internet Addiction Center.)

Among veteran trial lawyers, expert witnesses whose testimony could be the deciding factor in a close case were flavors of the month. They seemed to pop up on everyone's legal radar (in today's world, social media accounts) at the same time, triggering intense excitement and demand for their services, and then disappear with changing tastes.

"David Greenfield was the hottest thing in the world at the time," Sheffield recalled. "He had this internet clinic and was charging $600 an hour. Everybody wanted him."

Dr. Greenfield's evaluation began with a two-hour telephone interview on July 29. A follow-up, six-hour session was conducted at Seagoville on September 26, 2011. In the one-on-one interview, Greenfield not only noted Stan's physical disability—Stan used a walker to get around – but also another more troubling physical anomaly. Eye contact with his subject, he reported, became, "more sparse and difficult," as the session progressed. Given the significance of the interaction, one would imagine a "normal" person with so much at stake engaging more directly with his psychologist.

Greenfield reviewed Stan's voluminous psychiatric and medical records. He administered an autism evaluation survey hoping to diagnose Stan's thus far inexplicable blocking. He studied transcripts of the critical chats between Stan and other chat room denizens as well as the incriminating exchanges between Stan and Detective Spector.

■ ■ ■

Unlike Stan's previous lawyers, Sheffield stayed in constant contact with him. This was no small thing to a man in his precarious position. When he was en route to FCI Seagoville, she arranged to meet with him for a three-hour consultation while he was being held at the Atlanta federal penitentiary.

"One of Linda's greatest assets," he said, "is that she always explains things to me. She always answers the phone herself, and I have permission to phone her at any time I want her to understand that I'm not just #76042–004, but a human being with feelings, a family, and a prior life."

The Atlanta pen was a harrowing place with a history of riots and violence. Prisoners were locked in their cells twenty-three hours a day.

After meeting with Sheffield, the stress became so intense that Stan suffered what he later described as a "nervous breakdown." Rather than calming the distraught prisoner, the Bureau of Prisons psychologist who saw him glanced at his rap sheet and advised Stan that he needed to come up a more palatable backstory. Inmates, she told him, were known to torture and murder child molesters.

"To me, a former white-collar professional, this dungeon was beyond hell," Stan recalled. "No place could be more demoralizing, dehumanizing, and full of evil."

■ ■ ■

On October 10, 2011, Dr. Greenfield produced his long-awaited, fifty-page evaluation. It was not the game-changer Linda Sheffield was hoping for. What was needed was an insightful, cogent, fact-based argument explaining Stan's behavior as the extreme fantasies of a man who was ill and in need of help, not a guilty man. Sheffield believed there was more than ample information and data to support that conclusion.

Instead, Greenfield simply rehashed Stan's medical history, then diagnosed a series of underlying pathologies. None of it unlocked the disordered mind at the time of his arrest.

Greenfield determined that Stan's lifelong blocking (in concert with poor social judgment, anxiety, and other symptoms) was indicative of Asperger's Syndrome. Stan spoke "with little sense of intimate connection," Greenfield noted, "as if I were not there"—consistent with Asperger's. "He was narcissistic (Narcissistic Personality Disorder), which translates to his inflated sense of his own importance, arrogance, a lack of empathy, and a desperate need for admiration. Behind Rothenberg's mask lies a very fragile ego."

Doug Feldman had noticed his friend's unsettling behavior years before. He'd observed Rothenberg having problems interacting with people. "He literally couldn't tell what was totally right from what was wrong."

The larger point was that Stan Rothenberg, judgment hampered by Asperger's and engulfed in a benzodiazepine fog, was so lost in his fantasy world that he was totally unable "to adequately process information in those critical days leading up to his arrest." In Sheffield's view, this state of mind represented obvious grounds for judicial relief.

There were other significant points embedded in Greenfield's evaluation:

Based on previous sexual evaluations and my assessment, it was unlikely that Mr. Rothenberg would have actually performed a sex act with a child.

He was not a pedophile and does not derive primary sexual attraction from children.

Mr. Rothenberg gets off on shocking and using very overt sexual talk. This was his sexual arousal pattern.

He had a long history of homosexual promiscuity
where the line between fantasy and activity clearly
became blurred.

Greenfield concluded, rather feebly, that Stan's "method of self-medication was the use and abuse of the internet."

Ultimately, none of it mattered.

Judge Graham declined to grant Sheffield an evidentiary hearing. Dr. Greenfield's very expensive testimony and other arguments the attorney painstakingly gathered went unheard.

"The issue was never taken seriously by anybody," Sheffield said later. "Nobody was really listening to our argument that this wasn't real. I know the prosecutor wasn't listening. She thought it was a bunch of crap. And the judge did too. They all thought the case was disgusting.

"And it is. When you read the stuff, it was disgusting, but you know what? Fantasy is disgusting. Every single person in this world has disgusting fantasies. Stan's happened to come out in public. He was punished for having fantasies. People were afraid to call it what it was because it makes them look like they condone the reality of the fantasy."

As of 1987, there is no right of appeal after the denial of a federal habeas corpus petition. "I filed a request for a certificate of appealability to the Eleventh Circuit when the district court denied one, then went to the US Supreme Court when the Eleventh Circuit denied us. Lost there too," Sheffield said.

The Petition for a Writ may not have been successful, but Sheffield wasn't done. She had one last card to play and it was Stan's last chance to avoid spending the rest of his life in jail: a Petition for Compassionate Release.

PART IV

BACKLASH

Twenty-two

===

IN HIS CORNER of Florida, St. Lucie County Sheriff's Detective Neil Spector was *The Man* when it came to internet sex crime. It was Spector who singlehandedly sent Stan Rothenberg to prison for the rest of his life after one face-to-face meeting and a handful of instant messages and phone calls. When he encountered Rothenberg in the FamLuv chat room, the diminutive forty-three-year-old detective had worked on more than 200 child-exploitation and child pornography cases, taken part in myriad surveillance and sting operations, and reportedly dispatched scores of other men to long stretches in federal prison.

Spector operated under dozens of personas and screen names, patrolling the darkest corners of the internet, places where cyberspace and the most depraved human impulses intersect—websites that traffic in slavery, incest, bestiality, cruelty, and child abuse. Like the men he hunted, Spector was a stalker, concealed and patient, laying traps, setting up blinds and subterfuges to draw his prey into the light. Like them, he moved between two worlds—one noble and upstanding, the other tainted and corrupt—without becoming tainted himself.

Neil Spector's shining moment came when his dogged undercover police work delivered a dangerous Massachusetts child predator named Lonnie Waite to justice. Spector's performance was so outstanding that the Department of Justice named him a recipient of the 2009 Child Protection Award for "extraordinary efforts to protect children from harm."

That was a very big deal, particularly for a small and little-known sheriff's department on a Florida backwater. In Sheriff Ken Mascara's and the rest of his colleagues' eyes, Neil Spector was the toast of St. Lucie County. He flew to Washington, DC, for an awards banquet packed with fellow law enforcement officers, child protection advocates, and parents of missing and abducted children. Acting Assistant Attorney General Laurie Robinson, who emceed the affair, commended the honorees for acting "quickly and with a cool head to remove children from danger." Back in Florida, the sheriff department's Facebook page blossomed with images of Spector in his braided dress uniform surrounded by laughing celebrating colleagues.

A year later, in 2009, he screwed up. Big time. According to press reports (Spector did not return queries seeking comment), he found himself embroiled in an Internal Affairs investigation after state prosecutors complain he was making plea deals with defendants "outside the presence of the State Attorney's office."

The investigation revolved around an alleged relationship between Spector and Mark Coren, a defendant he arrested in 2008 on charges of "lewd computer solicitation of a child and lewd or lascivious exhibition." According to public records, sometime between Coren's arrest and subsequent plea bargain, Detective Spector and defense attorney Jay Kirschner allegedly "arrive at a suitable plea agreement" on their own. This occurred before a prosecutor was even assigned to Coren's case.

According to St. Lucie County Sheriff's Department Internal Affairs records, Spector allegedly recommended a sentencing cap of twenty-four months, one month less than the minimum sentence. State prosecutor Sandra Day wanted to send Coren to prison for four years. According to *TCPalm* reporter Will Greenlee (who was given access to the Internal Affairs report), when Prosecutor Day questioned Spector as to why Coren's sentence should be less than the minimum, Spector lamely argued prosecutors aren't "consistent with these cases." (If Coren had been convicted in the federal system rather than the state courts, his minimum sentence would have been ten years rather than two.)

To Prosecutor Day's astonishment, Spector then testified at Coren's bail hearing. He supported the defense attorney's motion for a lower bond. Day found herself thrust into a kind of *Alice In Wonderland* situation where black was white, up was down, and right was wrong, "a strange position I've never had to be in before," she said, "cross-examining law enforcement."

As part of the investigation, Lieutenant Larry Hostetler of the St. Lucie County Sherriff Department's contacted a second Florida prosecutor, Assistant State Attorney Robyn Stone. She made no bones about Spector's behavior: "To have a law enforcement officer come into open court in front of a judge on behalf of the defendant for the defense attorney, to me, it was just completely inappropriate and despicable."

In April 2008, Mark Coren was sentenced to thirty months in prison on each count, the sentences to run concurrently. Neil Spector showed up at the sentencing hearing and testified as a defense witness. A month later, Coren, still not satisfied with his kid gloves treatment, appealed.

Not long after, it came to light that Neil Spector had accepted a gift—two laptop computers—from Coren's defense attorney Jay Kirschner. According to Internal Affairs' records obtained by the *TCPalm* newspaper, Spector "concealed them from his immediate chain of command."

Five months later, Spector finally told his superiors about the computers. He described them as gifts to the department. Prosecutor Day said with much sarcasm that she was never heard of a case where a defendant purchased gifts for the sheriff's office.

"It was like buying off law enforcement," she complained to the Internal Affairs investigators. "It was not fair to the justice system. I mean you get somebody that has a lot of money that's going to get a better sentence."

■ ■ ■

Assistant US Attorney Rinku Talwar, who relied on Neil Spector's testimony in prosecuting Stanley Rothenberg, was taken aback. Approached as part of the Spector investigation, she told Lieutenant Hostetler, "(it) sounds like a bribe."

■ ■ ■

In the course of the probe, Spector admitted to the Internal Affairs officers that he'd been "stupid." He should have told his supervisors about the laptops. He denied doing "anything under the table."

On July 29, 2009, Detective Neil Spector was issued a formal reprimand by Sheriff Mascara. Mascara said Spector's outstanding record was a factor in determining a suitable punishment.

"This was a learning experience for the agency," Mascara said at the time. "We're not going to tolerate someone stepping out of our policies."

Spector stayed with the department for six more years, reportedly requesting a transfer to a "less stressful" bailiff's position. In January 2015, Sheriff Mascara and his colleagues gathered to fete him a final time at his retirement party. Someone posted images on the department's Facebook page of trays of pasta and a cake emblazoned with an American flag, all in all, a subdued sendoff. In 2016, Neil Spector was operating Spector Investigations, a private investigation firm in St. Lucie County.

Other than that one incident, Spector was never accused or charged with any wrongdoing. He retired with full honors.

Nonetheless, in the internet world where Spector spent so much of his career there was at least one anecdotal, albeit unconfirmed, story about what at best might be called hyper-aggressive policing. It was posted on the criminal law website (justanswer. com) by a person who claimed to be the mother of a young man Spector arrested in a sting operation. The circumstances of that arrest (including the meeting in a McDonald's parking

lot) exactly parallel what happened to Stanley Rothenberg after his chat room encounter with Neil Spector. All
the fear and emotional turmoil Rothenberg and his family
experienced, his confusion, and his legal missteps were
reflected in this woman's post. It has been lightly edited
for clarity and conciseness:

> *I know this sounds like it was coming from an irratio-
> nal parent.*
>
> *My son was arrested for soliciting a minor on the inter-
> net on July 2, 2009. He was now in Allenwood Low
> in PA.*
>
> *He was arrested by Neil Spector. . . . Mr. Spector was in
> an 18+ chat room looking for someone to sting. Yes, my
> son did chat with someone who claimed to be 15. He
> did go to the meeting place (McDonald's restaurant)
> but thought better of what he was doing and decided
> that he would not participate in the meeting the young
> woman set up for them.*
>
> *He was told that he was being arrested for loitering
> in the McDonald's parking lot. He was confused. He
> hadn't been there long and wasn't looking for a teen.
> Somehow Mr. Spector took the case federal. He called
> me and TOLD me not to post bail for my son because
> if the case went federal I would be wasting my money.*
>
> *I posted bail because I wanted to get my boy home so
> I could speak with him and take the appropriate next
> steps. When I posted bond my son was immediately
> taken to a drug and mental institution. This young*

man with no priors of any kind was taken without the appropriate paperwork to New Horizons Hospital. He was not released until July 7 when Mr. Spector showed up with a sealed Federal Arrest Warrant that no one could see—including my son. We were to take him at his word that there was a federal arrest warrant. Before I could get a good attorney my son was gone into the system. He found an attorney who seemed legitimately kind. My son believed that he would work on his best behalf so we hired him. I realize now that my son wanted so much to find an advocate that he was willing to believe anyone with a kind word.

He also believed Neil Spector when he said, "I'm here to help you. But I can only help you if you talk to me." Never having been arrested before, and going on Mr. Spector's kindness—also not knowing that his texted conversation was in fact with this very same 40+year-old man (Spector).

Not having made a legitimate phone call to me in 4 days. . . isolated from me (my son) needed someone to believe in…. The entire case escaped like a runaway train. By October, he had been convinced to plead guilty. To seem like he was assisting in his own conviction he elaborated in his confession to some things that weren't necessarily all true.

We all screw up. There were so many others who were actually involved with real children who were serving 3 years. My son was serving 10 years with lifetime probation for talking to a 40-year-old man acting like a young woman and never put a finger on any child. . .

So there was no trial even though my son wanted one.
He now sits in prison and would be wonderful asset to
his community—has always been.

I know, I know. . . all mothers say this about their chil-
dren. . .

■ ■ ■

No one can fault Neil Spector for working on sting operations. He proved himself one of the very best operators,
bringing men who preyed on society's most vulnerable
to justice. Stings were also high-profile, much-publicized,
unambiguous-seeming, and often career-enhancing operations that garner TV coverage and newspaper headlines
along the lines of "The Largest DEA Drug Bust in History"
or the "Massive Weapons Cache" seized by ATF agents or

"Man sentenced to twenty-five years after caught in
Port St. Lucie child porn sting"

That man was Stanley Rothenberg, and that's a real
headline from the December 8, 2008, edition of the
TCPalm newspaper, part of the *USA Today* chain. By
then, a lot more was known about him and the unhappy
circumstances that led him to show up at a McDonald's
parking lot on that fateful May afternoon.

Rothenberg was busted during a months-long, multi-
agency sting called Operation Safe Summer. Twenty-seven
other men were arrested along with him and charged
"soliciting children for sex," "traveling to meet children for
sex," and "downloading and trading child pornography."
One of these men, a fisherman named Charles Giovinco,
reportedly offered Neil Spector (rehashing his incestuous
father role) a catch of spiny lobsters and diving lessons in

payment for sex with Spector's purported eleven-year-old daughter.

Rothenberg's twenty-five-year (300 months) sentence was greater by far than the average sentence for murder (252 months), kidnapping (197 months), robbery and arson (77 months), drug trafficking (68 months), and manslaughter (60 months). It was actually more severe than the average sentence for contact sexual abuse offense, including child solicitation.

■ ■ ■

Successful stings were the Academy Awards of police work. During sting operations, undercover agents engage in the same behaviors, dealing drugs or guns or human trafficking, as the criminals they were pursuing. This creates the potential for entrapment and outright corruption. Hollywood churns out films depicting clever, courageous, tortured, or dishonest cops in these deceptions, such as *The Departed*, one of the more recent, and *The Sting*, the best-known. A movie about entrapment?

Not so much.

■ ■ ■

In the last years, a few district judges have begun to look more closely at sting operations denouncing some of them as "entrapment" and even "made-up crimes." Drawing particular judicial ire have been so-called stash house robberies—stings set up by the US Bureau of Alcohol, Tobacco, Firearms and Explosives (ATF). In these operations, undercover ATF agents offer their targets, typically known criminals, enormous payoffs to rob what were nonexistent drug stash houses. When the heavily armed robbers appear on scene, they are arrested and charged with multiple felonies—convictions that carry long prison sentences. The ATF defends these fictional robberies as effective ways of removing violent criminals from the streets.

In 2014, California District Court Judge Otis D. Wright II pushed back, throwing out all charges against Antonio Dunlap, a man arrested by the ATF in Los Angeles during a stash house sting. Wright found no evidence that Dunlap had been involved in drug house robberies in the past and no indication he would have participated if the undercover ATF agent had not offered him the chance.

"Society does not win when the government stoops to the same level as the defendants it seeks to prosecute," Judge Wright complained, "especially when the government had acted solely to achieve a conviction in a made up crime."

Wright also complained such stings do little to deter crime. Instead they "ensnare chronically unemployed individuals from poverty-stricken areas." A 2013 *USA Today* investigation supported Wright's objections. "The time had come to remind the Executive Branch that the Constitution charges it with law enforcement, not crime creation," Wright continued.

A second California judge, US District Judge Manuel Real, dismissed stash house robbery charges against three men who'd already pleaded guilty. Judge Real found that undercover ATF agents had "created a fictitious crime from whole cloth."

As stings expand and proliferate into other areas of law enforcement and sentences become too onerous to sustain, other jurists were beginning to balk at what they see as unjustified prosecutions. "They were getting really frustrated," said Katherine Tinto, a Benjamin N. Cardozo School of Law professor, "by not being given sufficient answers on how these people were targeted."

As Judge Wright phrases it, "A reverse sting operation transcends the bounds of due process and makes the government the oppressor."

Twenty-three

INMATES FIFTY YEARS of age and older were the fastest-growing population in already overcrowded federal correctional institutions. From 2009 to 2013, the number of elderly prisoners increased by 25 percent to more than thirty-one thousand, another unintended consequence of decades of draconian sentencing policies. Inmate healthcare costs now run $1 billion annually; administrators are being forced to set up geriatric wards and sophisticated chronic care facilities to deal with the depredations of old age. Costly prescription drugs, upgraded treatment, dental and medical needs, even hospice service, have driven the cost of housing one elderly prisoner to $60,000 annually. By comparison, incarceration costs for a general population inmate run $27,000.

All this expense and a growing debate over the purpose of even keeping the vast majority of these old men behind bars was unfolding against a backdrop of penny-pinching congressional watchdogs, slashed funding, and budget shortfalls.

"Federal prisons were starting to resemble nursing homes surrounded with razor wire," said Julie Stewart, president of Families Against Mandatory Minimums (FAMM), a national organization working to reform mandatory minimum sentencing. "It makes no sense fiscally or from the perspective of human compassion to incarcerate men and women who pose no threat to public safety and who have long since paid for their crime."

In 2013, Department of Justice Inspector General (IG) Glen Fine released a scathing report criticizing the tail dragging of the Bureau of Prisons that led to the deaths of sick and elderly prisoners who, in many cases, spent years awaiting decisions on so-called compassionate release petitions. Astonishingly, in five years (2006 to 2011), the BOP Central Office approved fewer than two dozen compassionate release petitions. More than twice as many (twenty-eight) prisoners literally died awaiting word. The IG report detailed what amounts to a systematic refusal to process these claims: in five years, prison wardens and BOP regional offices around the nation forwarded only 211 compassionate requests to the central office for consideration.

In a 2013 speech before the American Bar Association, Attorney General Eric Holder gave voice to these concerns, calling for an end to mandatory minimums that condemn nonviolent offenders to long prison terms that do not serve society's interests. Almost half were serving time for drug-related crimes in a system that was 40 percent over capacity. Holder also pushed for the early release of seniors and seriously ill inmates who pose no danger to society.

"While the aggressive enforcement of federal criminal statutes remains necessary," Holder said, "we cannot simply prosecute or incarcerate our way to becoming a safer nation. We must never stop being tough on crime. But we must also be smarter on crime."

At seventy-three, Stanley Rothenberg seemed to fit Holder's depiction precisely. Never violent or predatory, he was in ill health, and his "debt" to society such as it is, had long been paid. He has surrendered his freedom, his home, his fortune, his good name, and what may well be the final years of his life.

■ ■ ■

In the spring of 2016, Matthew Norman, MD, a board-certified forensic psychiatrist and neurologist (specializing in disorders affecting the brain, spinal cord, and nerves) undertook a thorough review of Stanley Rothenberg's long history of medical and psychiatric illness and his ongoing struggle with more than a dozen physiological ills. These were exacerbated, Norman noted, to the point of debilitation by Rothenberg's overarching anxiety and the lack of adequate medical care for geriatric patients in the BOP system.

Dr. Norman's medical review alone ran ten single-spaced pages. Among other things, he noted that some of Rothenberg's medical prescriptions had seemingly been dispensed without adequate regard for so-called "contraindications," i.e., harmful reactions when taken in conjunction with other medications. In effect, his medicine was making him sick. Ironically, Rothenberg had also had a BOP doctor *take away* medication when he challenged a reduced dosage that did little to bring his anxiety under control.

Norman described Rothenberg's ongoing arteriosclerotic vascular disease (ASVD) as "life-threatening," citing numerous prior studies that describe plaque buildup on the walls of his arteries. He warned that Rothenberg was increasingly likely to suffer a catastrophic stroke or heart attack unless action was taken to bring his stress under control.

The psychiatric review documents more than forty years of treatment with psychotherapy and habit-forming benzo-diazepines. Norman diagnosed Rothenberg with depression, generalized anxiety disorder (persistent debilitating anxiety characterized by restlessness, fatigue, sleeplessness, irrita-bility, and the inability to concentrate) and, at the same time, narcissistic personality disorder, which made him desper-ate for admiration and importance.

Given this history, the SSA declared Rothenberg dis-abled in 2002. Since his conviction and incarceration, the BOP had essentially ignored his psychiatric issues and left him untreated by either effective therapy or ade-quate pharmacological intervention. Norman described Rothenberg as living in a constant state of "severe agita-tion" far beyond the prison system's ability to address. In effect, Stanly Rothenberg was facing yet another tragedy.

Yet the BOP psychiatrists consistently labeled Rothen-berg, "drug-seeking" and "feigning illness." Norman argued that Rothenberg was in such life-threatening dis-tress, they should bypass their own formulary restrictions and put the man back on benzodiazepines to save his life.

If anything, Norman's comprehensive medical and psychological assessment, buttressed by an increasing body of research, suggested that Stanley G. Rothenberg would pose no threat to anyone, ever. In 2011, Peter Briggs, Walter Simon, and Stacy Simonsen published "An Explor-atory Study of Internet-Initiated Sexual Offenses and the Chat Room Sex Offender" (*Sexual Abuse: A Journal of Research and Treatment, March 2011).* Their research, drawn from interviews with more than fifty online sex offenders, 90 percent of whom were arrested in internet sex stings, suggest that men like Rothenberg were "only driven by online sexual fantasies and would not have progressed to an in-person sexual assault."

The researchers also suggested that Internet chat room sex offenders were a distinct group, characterized by backgrounds and experiences less likely to lead to criminal behavior than contact sex offenders. Ninety percent of the men in the study were not diagnosed as pedophiles. Dr. David Greenfield of the Center for Internet and Technology Addiction came to the same conclusion after interviewing Rothenberg: He was no pedophile. The remainder of the 2011 study might have been lifted from the pages of a diary documenting Stanley Rothenberg's later life: chat room sex offenders "avoid relationships; they spent a significant amount of time in online chat rooms as a primary social and sexual outlet; they engage in other sexually compulsive behaviors."

■ ■ ■

Stan's connections to family and friends grew tenuous. Only his attorney, Linda Sheffield, his sister, Gail, brother-in-law, Joel, and a few stalwart friends regularly stayed in touch. The lush and luxurious garden of personal, business, and community relationships he so carefully cultivated had withered. With the prospect of a compassionate release far from assured, he faced a final indignity: growing feeble and dying in prison.

There are tens of thousands like him, old men in whom the recklessness, addiction, and frustration that fueled their antisocial behavior had long been burned away in the penitentiaries. Their fate, to die alone and unredeemed, is the bitter harvest of decades of politically-driven demands for mandatory minimum and extreme sentencing. Like Rothenberg, the majority of these aging prisoners were not—and never were—violent. Ironically, it was society that was visiting violence upon them.

Twenty-four

SPRING CAME EARLY to central Texas. The air was cool and fragrant, the heat and humidity of the long summer briefly at bay. Bluebonnets, poppies, primrose, verbena, Indian Blanket, and other wildflowers painted the fields outside the walls of FCI Seagoville. Inside the prison, there were no seasons. Nature itself was held captive—the bushes and hedges fiercely trimmed and shaped, rose bushes neatly planted, descendants perhaps of those planted by Japanese gardeners interned and imprisoned at the same site by the US government seventy-five years prior. The air was ripe with the aroma of 1,800 men living in extremely close quarters amidst an endless cacophony of television, radio, shouting, and grating PA system announcements.

The Seagoville compound had a long, unhappy history. Originally constructed as a women's reformatory, it was transformed in the early 1940s into an internment camp for the Nisei, first-generation Japanese-Americans, and their immigrant parents (Issei) who were deemed

237

"enemy aliens" in the hysteria following the attack on Pearl Harbor. Postwar, the compound was reconverted into a juvenile hall for criminal adolescents and finally, a low-security prison. FCI Seagoville was one of nine federal institutions housing sex offender treatment programs and had an inmate population that reflected this focus.

■ ■ ■

Stan arrived on February 24, 2011, after a disheartening weeks-long detour at the nightmarish Atlanta federal pen. From Atlanta, he flew via commuter airline (inmates cynically label the service "ConAir") to Texarkana, Arkansas, and then on to Oklahoma City. There he left his cane on the plane, realized he had a long way to walk in handcuffs and shackles, and asked a corrections officer to have the cane retrieved from the overhead compartment.

"Keep moving!" the man warned.

Rothenberg made it to a wooden bench and refused, amid a chorus of shouts, to get up. It was not an auspicious arrival. He was sixty-seven years old. Worsening polyneuropathy—nerve damage characterized by weakness, numbness, a pins-and needles sensation, and pain—forced him to rely on the cane to get around. From Oklahoma City he traveled by bus—handcuffed and shackled to Seagoville.

At Seagoville, he was assigned to Housing Unit 7, an original two-story cellblock (original in that it lacks air-conditioning and handicap access, a growing problem given the rapidly aging inmate population in federal prisons). Industrial fans lined the corridors, but the inmates slept in cells that registered one hundred degrees in the summer. They were forced to rely on fans that had to be purchased at the commissary.

Given his condition, a sympathetic prison physician transferred Rothenberg to Unit 54, a newer open-design, air-conditioned building with the handicap accessible toilets and showers he requires.

At 6'5" and 180 pounds, Prisoner #76042–004 hardly projected the stereotype muscled jailhouse gangbanger with "love" and "hate" tattooed on his knuckles. Reticent, bookish, overeducated (compared to his inmate peers), and determined to keep a lifeline to the outside world, he quickly decided to spend as much time as he could in Seagoville's law and leisure libraries, reading, researching, and pounding out letters and emails on the computers in the learning center. Federal inmates can send and receive email under a closely supervised CorrLinks system. (Access to the internet was blocked.)

By 2016, he'd stepped into a role with which he was entirely comfortable: social activist. Stan subscribed to twelve to fifteen newspapers and magazines so he could stay current on the outside world. When he came across interesting or timely articles, he copied and distributed them to interested inmates as well as to his circle of family and friends, attorney Linda Sheffield, and the occasional judge, prison reform advocate, or elected official. The key was keeping busy.

"If I owe letters to anybody, I type them up," he said. "If I have any photocopying to do, I take care of that."

As a low-security facility, Seagoville offered inmates what the Bureau of Prisons described as educational, vocational training, and leisure programs. The classroom courses offered include many taught by inmates, not exactly the cream of the educational system. After settling in, Rothenberg dutifully enrolled in a few of them. He completed the work but left disappointed and unfulfilled.

"I found the experience so dismal," he said, "I never went back."

Dismal was the operative word.

Stan's scheduled release date is 2030. He will be eighty-seven years old.

He has exhausted his appeals, and his only hope of getting out of prison is for compassionate release based on his age and deteriorating health.

Time weighed on him so heavily that he felt he couldn't come up for air. He spent his days desperately filling up the interminable hours.

While other men his age were spending their remaining years retired and "off-the-clock," Stanley's life was more regimented and disciplined than that of an army private suffering through basic training. Weekday mornings, he was awakened at 6:00 a.m. by the shrill, incomprehensible blast of the prison's PA system. On Mondays, visitation started at 8:30 a.m., with the garbled announcements running on interminably, naming every inmate who had a spouse or family member visit them. In Texas, Rothenberg's visitors were few and far between.

Every morning, emerging stiffly from his lower bunk, Rothenberg walked sleepily to the first-floor bathroom to pee and brush his teeth. In street shoes and a khaki uniform, he avoided the "light breakfast" being served in the chow hall and made his way using his walker to the Pill Line in Building 9 for his daily meds. Many of the men around him were former drug abusers, dealers, and scammers. The line format kept them from stealing medications from weaker inmates to "hustle" or ingest.

Returning to his cell, Rothenberg slipped on headphones and squinted at one of the three nearby TV sets mounted on the far wall hoping to catch *New Day*, CNN's morning news show. In the upside-down world of prison, groups of inmates controlled the televisions: the black prisoners had three, the Mexicans, and the white "hater" groups like the Aryan Brotherhood each had one. In 2016, the sex offenders were deemed either worthy or populous enough to be granted a TV of their own.

There was a hierarchy built into the seating around each TV set as well. "I must sit in the back of the viewing area," Rothenberg explained, "because privileged inmates claim they own the real estate close to the TVs. God forbid someone took one of these spots, even if there's no one there."

Tuesdays through Friday mornings, after absorbing the news headlines, he wrapped a long sock around his head, popped in ear plugs, and tried to grab an extra hour's sleep. That, too, was more complicated than an elderly man stealing a needed nap. Demons shouted pain, guilt, and loss in his head. His legs ached from permanent anxiety caused by too many benzo withdrawals. His existence was utterly wretched. Drifting off to sleep is hardly a given.

At 10:00 a.m., he was up for the day. He treated himself to an eighteen-ounce mug of iced coffee, a habit he picked up from Joe Rothenberg a lifetime ago.

"What I miss most from my prior life," he said, "are Dunkin' Donuts iced coffee and homegrown Hanover tomatoes from Virginia."

He strolled over to the housing unit computer, checked his mail and prison announcements, and listened to a few snippets of songs on his MP3 player, and occasionally purchased one if it grabbed him. He bought mostly oldies from the '60s, but increasingly the desolate attraction—loneliness, heartache, betrayal—of country music.

"Most country DJs were not gay-friendly," he said, "but

that hasn't stopped me from listening. I've discovered that the lyrics were actually decipherable." A good thing, because at that point so little in Stan's life was comprehensible.

At 10:30 a.m., the inmates drifted back to the housing unit and waited to be released to the chow hall. Rothenberg usually passed on lunch, opting for a Cup O' Soup, granola bar, or a package of Ritz peanut butter crackers he kept in his locker. At one time he might have made fruit salad, but the fresh grapefruit he used to get was no longer given to inmates. Inmates were discovered fermenting the fruit to distill homemade hooch.

"The quality of the food in the chow hall had deteriorated tremendously, and the preparation was hit or miss," he said.

So bad that he restarted his gadfly food critiques, this time scrutinizing Ms. White, Seagoville's temporary food service administrator.

"My work was not official business," he admitted, "but I keep pressure on her to prepare our meals just as they were advertised per the BOP national menu."

After a year, he said, "The only thing I've been successful with was getting butter pats distributed at every meal. No exceptions. Yawn."

When he was done working on the computer in the law library—usually late afternoon—Stan returned to his cell to read. He found a good buddy and a formidable Scrabble opponent in Jake, a young sex offender (severely over-sentenced) for a non-touching crime. Jake, a college grad, was working on a master's degree via correspondence classes.

"We began bonding soon after he arrived in 2013," Rothenberg said. "Jake was a liberal on social issues as I am and can commiserate with me."

On Mondays and Tuesdays, the two met in the law library to "catch up on prison drama and personal thoughts not generally shared with others." On Sundays, the two headed out to the recreation yard and played 4–5 games of competitive Scrabble.

"We were like two dogs in a cat fight," Stan said. Jake usually won.

Jake had spent the last sixteen months awaiting word on a habeas corpus petition (arguing his sentence amounts to cruel and unusual punishment in violation of the constitution). In the process, Jake's mother, who had become a prison reform advocate and a good friend, mailed Stan copies of web-based articles he found interesting and informative.

At 2:50 p.m., recreation time ended. Each inmate returned to his cell for the mandatory 4:00 p.m. count. The counts were done twice daily, three times on weekends and holidays. Then it was mail call, with all incoming mail opened and inspected for contraband. Any intended recipient of contraband—knowingly or unknowingly—was subject to disciplinary action.

At dinnertime, Rothenberg usually avoided the chow hall, preferring to fix something healthy and light, maybe an egg salad (hard-boiled eggs smuggled out of the chow hall cost thirty cents or a postage stamp) or a faux chicken salad he made using packets of pre-cooked chicken purchased in the commissary, mayo, and relish. He usually tried to catch the afternoon news broadcast on KRLD, the Dallas/Fort Worth AM radio station.

■ ■ ■

On April 11, 2016, Rothenberg's seventy-third birthday passed unnoticed in FCI Seagoville. It was his ninth year of incarceration, his sixth in Texas.

In those nine years, Stanley Rothenberg, lifelong upstanding citizen turned convicted felon, has done penance for his sins and paid his debt to society many times over. Now with the prospect of a compassionate release far from assured, he faces the prospect of growing old and dying in prison—a death sentence by any measure.

A Petition for Compassionate Release is an interesting procedural method of dealing with the increasing elderly population. It's governed by 18 USC. §§ 3582(c)(1)(A) and 4205(g).

§571.60 Purpose and scope. Under 18 USC 4205(g), a sentencing court, on motion of the Bureau of Prisons, may make an inmate with a minimum term sentence immediately eligible for parole by reducing the minimum term of the sentence to time served. Under 18 USC 3582(c)(1)(A), a sentencing court, on motion of the Director of the Bureau of Prisons, may reduce the term of imprisonment of an inmate sentenced under the Comprehensive Crime Control Act of 1984. The Bureau uses 18 USC 4205(g) and 18 USC 3582(c)(1)(A) in particularly extraordinary or compelling circumstances which could not reasonably have been foreseen by the court at the time of sentencing.

For the purposes of this Program Statement, the terms "compassionate release" and "reduction in sentence" are used interchangeably.

In deciding whether to file a motion under either 18 USC 4205(g) or 18 USC 3582(c)(1)(A), the Bureau of Prisons should consider whether the inmate's release would pose a danger to the safety of any other person or the community.

Stan would fall under subsection b.

b. Elderly Inmates with Medical Conditions. Inmates who fit the following criteria:

- Age sixty-five and older.

- Suffer from chronic or serious medical conditions related to the aging process.

- Experiencing deteriorating mental or physical health that substantially diminishes their ability to function in a correctional facility.

- Conventional treatment promises no substantial improvement to their mental or physical condition.

- Have served at least 50 percent of their sentence.

Additionally, for inmates in this category, the BOP should consider the following factors when evaluating the risk that an elderly inmate may reoffend:

- The age at which the inmate committed the current offense.

- Whether the inmate suffered from these medical conditions at the time the inmate committed the offense.

- Whether the inmate suffered from these medical conditions at the time of sentencing and whether the Presentence Investigation Report (PSR) mentions these conditions.

The BOP Medical Director will develop and issue medical criteria to help evaluate the inmate's suitability for consideration under this RIS category.

The compassionate release process begins with the inmate filing a request with the warden of his current institution, requesting consideration for compassionate release or reduction in sentence. The request goes through two stages of review by the warden. If the warden decides the request has merit, the warden then files a petition with the court that originally sentenced the defendant.

For Stan, if the warden at Seagoville approves his request, that means the petition will be filed with the original judge who sentenced him to effectively a life sentence for talking dirty on the internet. This is Stan's last chance to avoid dying in prison. At seventy-five years of age, infirm and barely mobile, he poses no danger to society.

In fact, Stan's story could end something like this . . .

The Final Chapter

STAN STEPPED OUT into the cool spring air, marveling at how the light breeze felt on his skin. He'd waited for this moment for so long, imagining how it would feel. Fresh air, sunlight, nothing filtered through the gray bars and cement of prison. The stink of cement, Pine Sol over filth, the constant echo and routines. In his dreams, he'd imagined the emotional equivalent of a band playing, crowds cheering, and fireworks.

The weeks leading up to his release had been more tedious than even some parts of prison. So many forms to fill out! Waivers, disclaimers, agreements that he barely understood, conditions of parole, handouts on adapting to the world, counseling sessions on his reentry into society—all disruptions to his routine.

The routine. That's what had kept him sane while in prison. Friends, a few small luxuries, and the routine—that's all there was. Now, even with the prospect of complete freedom, the disruption in his routine was unsettling.

Craziness. All leading up to this very moment.

He paused for a moment just inside the door, relishing the thrill of anticipation. Anticipation—and yet, a bit of nervousness. Anxiety boiled just below the surface, tight across his chest, grinding deep in his guts.

On one level, leaving prison seemed like no big deal, everything he'd always wanted. Or at least everything he'd wanted for the last ten years.

But now, with it right in front of him, he felt the oddest, most distasteful bit of reluctance. And he hated that he felt the least bit reluctant. What really was out there waiting for him? Could he have a good life again?

Calm down. Just calm down. It will be all right.

Taking a deep breath, he pushed open the door, and stepped out into the sunshine.

■ ■ ■

"Stan!" Gail Lewis spotted her brother the moment he stepped out and darted over to wrap him in a rib-cracking hug. Her husband, Joel, was just half a step behind her. Together they enveloped Stan and held him tight.

"You're too thin," Gail said finally, her voice slightly unsteady. She held him tight, surprised at how frail he felt, and a wave of protectiveness swept over her. This was her blood, her family, and nothing in the world would ever change that. She pulled back from him slightly and stared up at him. "It's so good to see you. Oh, Stan . . ." Her voice broke.

"It's great to see you, Stan," Joel said, with one arm around Gail and another around Stan's shoulders. "Just great." They stood that way a few moments longer, giddy with happiness. It was over, all over—the lawyers, the prison, the constant worry about how Stan was holding up.

Stan was out. Stan was okay. In that moment, that was all that mattered.

■ ■ ■

Not now. Please don't let me start blocking. Enveloped by his family, emotions surging high, Stan took a deep breath and waited. As the second ticked by, he was relieved to find that he could still understand every word, follow every sentence. He let his breath out slowly, grateful for the small reprieve. Maybe this was the start of a new life. Just maybe.

He had a sudden flash of insight, realizing that he didn't really know how hard it had been on them, but that he suspected he would find out. But within moments that faded, and the reality of freedom rushed back in, overwhelming him.

"Let's get out of here," Joel said. He led the way over to the car. As they approached, Stan hesitated. Choices—he had choices—the first of many. Should he sit in the front seat next to Joel? Or would Gail be driving? Should she sit in the back with him, or should he sit in the front, and she would sit in the back. Surely they didn't expect him to drive, did they? Suddenly, the fact that he now had choices seemed a bit more daunting.

"Why don't you sit up front with Joel?" Gail said, obviously sensing his confusion. "I'll sit in the back so I can stretch out a bit."

"You're sure?" Stan asked, surprised to find his voice a little rusty.

Gail nodded. "We're very glad you're out, Stan. Very glad." She touched his arm briefly then slid into the back seat.

Stan opened the door and got into the car. He carefully buckled his seatbelt, adjusting the shoulder harness to a more comfortable position. How long had it been since he'd had to do this?

"We've got your room at the Radisson next to us," Joel said, speaking easily and naturally, trying to make Stan feel more comfortable. "I have the doctor's appointment set up, too." He shot a glance over at Stan. "Let's get that squared away first thing tomorrow morning, okay? Are you all right for tonight?"

Stan cleared his throat. "Yes, thank you. I'm okay tonight." His voice shook just the tiniest bit.

Even more important than being released from the confines of prison was the ability he now had to get back on his medications. In prison, he'd never once managed to get his doses quite right. He fought crippling anxiety, spiraling out of control, and lived with daily dread and depression, exacerbated by so many of the common consequences of aging. He'd survived with the support and encouragement of his friends and minimal doses of medication that muted the anxiety only so very slightly.

To be free of the anxiety, of the blocking, of the constant black cloud—that would be enough. The possibility that he could actually be happy never even crossed his mind.

■ ■ ■

The next few days flew by in a flurry of activity. Stan found the return to life outside prison overwhelming, and Joel and Gail quickly learned to recognize the signs. They planned their activities in shorter bursts, controlling the environment more carefully, making sure he was not stressed.

The first stop was for new clothes. Stan was tempted to splurge a little, but a lifetime of being cost-conscious and the overwhelming number of choices conspired against him. He liked the feel of natural fabrics, the higher-quality cottons and linens he'd been accustomed to before. What a relief it was to have shoes that fit finally, with good quality socks that stayed up and didn't pool around his ankles. The shoes were exquisite, so comfortable—he'd forgotten what it felt like to walk on air. And the styles—well, what many saw as subtle fashion changes year to year were an abrupt departure if you'd been locked up for ten years.

Often, as they stood waiting for service, Stan found himself slipping his fingers inside the waistband of his pants. It was what they were required to do in prison, keep their hands tucked in, not reaching out to other people.

The first week of freedom, he made himself break that habit, as well as countless other small survival habits he picked up. Gradually, his appetite picked up, and he delighted in rediscovering the classic dishes he'd missed and then forgotten. His cheeks swelled up a bit more, the hollows and planes of his face gently filling out. Within the first few weeks, the waistbands on his newly purchased wardrobe were tighter.

The days flew by, and his sense of belonging to the world increased every hour. With his mind now back under control with the correct pharmaceuticals, the possibility of a future became more and more real. Yes, he might be seventy-five years old, but he wasn't dead yet, was he? With access to modern medicine now, with the wonders of ED treatments, he even felt like it might be possible to—

No. his mind snapped away from the possibilities. Then he relaxed. This wasn't prison. He was allowed to have sexual fantasies, a life. All of that. For the first time, he considered the possibility of being happy.

■ ■ ■

The first year flew by, each day sweeter than the last. The sheer luxury of comfortable shoes and well-fitting socks finally started to fade—not completely, but just a bit. Each day brought more confidence; each month his horizons expanded.

He wrote about his experiences, both in prison and on transitioning to life outside of prison. He wrote for his friends and acquaintances in prison to let them know what it was really like to get out, where the Bureau of Prisons' literature was wrong and where it was right. He wrote for the families and friends of those still incarcerated, helping them to make sense of it and teaching them how to understand what their loved ones were going through on reentry. Finally, he wrote because it was the right thing to do, to challenge the status quo to improve conditions for everyone, to try to change laws and policies so that no one else would go through what he'd been through.

Soon the communities devoted to these issues were seeking him out, asking him to serve on committees and advisory boards. Reluctantly at first, Stan stepped back into the public arena, spurred by his sense of duty to his community. The facts of his case became common knowledge, how he'd been entrapped and convicted, which gave him additional credibility. He was surprised—and not surprised, because hadn't he been an innocent at one time himself?—at how little people knew about life in prison.

At first uncomfortable with his growing public notoriety, Stan came to see it as a tool. How he'd been treated was unconscionable in any civilized society. Entrapped, imprisoned for a pre-invented crime committed against a victim who did not exist—this was not how America should be. This was not a justice system but an interlocking web of deceptions and lies justified by out-of-control political correctness.

It wasn't right.

At an age when most men would have settled into a quiet retirement, Stanley G. Rothenberg was just getting started. He stepped into the battle for social justice with renewed vigor, the fire burning brightly in his heart. No one should have to suffer as he'd suffered, no one. It was time to put a stop to people like Neil Spector and the agencies that let them ruin lives.

■ ■ ■

No, this ending to Stan's story is not true.

Not yet.

BUT IT COULD BE.

■ ■ ■

Epilogue

AS OF THIS writing, Stanley G. Rothenberg is awaiting a decision from the Bureau of Prisons on his request for a Petition for Compassionate Release. As his case progresses, the briefs and documents will be available on the website: *https://justiceforstanrothenberg.com*

Appendix: Current Trends in Sentencing Law

A YEAR AFTER Stanley Rothenberg's appeal was rejected by the Eleventh Circuit, an enterprising Duke University law school student named Kory Christiansen took a closer look at the case. In 2011, his findings were published in a well-reasoned, thirty-three-page *Duke Law Review* article titled "Reforming Attempt Liability Under 18 USC. § 2422 (B): An Insubstantial Step Back From *United States v. Rothenberg*."

Christiansen cited a number of troubling legal issues raised by the Rothenberg prosecution. Simply put, he argued that Rothenberg was overcharged and over-sentenced and that the appellate court's inconsistent and flawed analysis of precedent aggravated rather than ameliorated the injustice. Worse, Christiansen suggested the Rothenberg ruling lowered the bar for additional overly-broad and aggressive prosecutions under so-called attempt liability laws.

Law review articles are research documents, filled with citations and often dry analysis. Despite that, like many articles, Christiansen tackled an important question: Will

the public's demand for preventative law enforcement to
protect children from internet predators trigger an unjust
violation of First Amendment guarantees by punishing
mere thoughts?

Citing *Rothenberg* and other cases prosecuted under
"attempt liability" statutes, Christiansen argued in the
affirmative. (The efficacy of such laws which were often
rooted in the widely disseminated, but flawed belief that
child molesters running rampant on the internet were
also targeting flesh-and-blood children in schoolyards
and playgrounds, was addressed in Chapter XXVI.)

The federal "attempt liability" statute, 18 USC. §2422 (b)
states, "Whoever, using the mail or any facility or means
of interstate or foreign commerce…knowingly persuades,
induces, entices or coerces any individual who had not
attained the age of eighteen years, to engage in prostitution or any sexual activity for which any person can be
charged with a criminal offense, or attempts to do so, shall
be fined and imprisoned not less than 10 years or for life."

"Attempts to do so" is a phrase rife with uncertainty.
How should prosecutors, juries, and judges determine
whether an attempt to persuade, induce, entice, or coerce
actually occurred? In other words, how can they tell
whether a crime has been committed when the wording
of the statute is so vague?

That wasn't the first statute that had tried to criminal-
ize "attempt liability." Christiansen argued that in previous
statutes, at least one of four elements had to be satisfied:

Whether a defendant's sexually explicit communications were sent directly to someone he believed was a
minor, or to an adult intermediary whose independent
cooperation would be required to complete the underlying crime;

Whether the defendant made sufficiently firm plans to meet the other party in the internet communication;

Whether the defendant took any other overt acts toward persuading, inducing, enticing, or coercing a minor;

Whether the defendant intended to engage personally in illicit sexual activity.

In any criminal trial, each element of a crime has to be proved beyond a reasonable doubt, and that includes the requirement that the defendant had taken a "substantial step" beyond mere preparation. For example, in *United States v. Resendiz-Ponce*, an immigration ruling overturned by the US Supreme Court, the majority noted in passing "that the mere intent to violate a federal criminal statute was not punishable as an attempt unless it was also accompanied by significant conduct." At the time, Justice Antonin Scalia went further, arguing that the word "attempt" does not necessarily imply an action that would constitute a substantial step.

Around 2004, Christiansen argued, the Eleventh Circuit began recasting the definition of substantial step. He cited a series of rulings in cases involving convicted sex offenders: In *United States v. Murrell*, for example, the Eleventh Circuit became the first federal appellate court to affirm a 2422 (b) conviction based on a defendant's interaction with a person he believed to be an adult. (In prior cases, undercover officers had assumed the personas of minor children.)

Like Stanley Rothenberg, Anthony Murrell (screen name Bone 1031) visited the AOL FamLuv chat room where he encountered an undercover detective posing as a father willing to "rent" his underage child for sex. Murrell again contacted the same purported father in

RentFVryYng, another member-created AOL chat room. He arranged to meet father and daughter at a local Holiday Inn and arrived with the agreed-upon $300 fee, a box of condoms, and a teddy bear for his victim. Murrell was arrested, charged, and convicted in district court in Port St. Lucie, Florida, the same court and the same detective, Neil Spector, who busted Stanley Rothenberg.

After reviewing Murrell's argument that communicating solely with individuals he believed were adults was not sufficient to trigger "attempt liability," the court agreed that Murrell had demonstrated "specific intent," and had taken a "substantial step" toward commission of the crime. Murrell's conviction was sustained.

In 2007, *United States v. Yost*, the Eleventh Circuit reviewed Jon Yost's contention that his actions did not constitute the substantial step required in 2422 (b) prosecutions. A resident of Dahlonega, a town in the north Georgia mountains, Yost had gone much further in his actions and "expressed intent" than Stanley Rothenberg. The gist of Yost's defense was that while he did arrange to meet a purported minor at a specific place and time for a sexual encounter, he failed to show up.

(By contrast, Stan had always insisted he'd traveled to meet the undercover detective, Spector, the purported father of the child, merely to "talk dirty" and decide whether he'd go further. Spector acknowledged this, even testifying, "The defendant indicated he was not sure if he actually would have had sex with the child.")

Jon Yost had telephoned "Lynn," an undercover agent he believed was a thirteen-year-old girl; he'd posted a picture of his genitalia online for her to view and made arrangements to meet her. There was no evidence that he'd made any attempt to travel to the assignation.

Nonetheless, the circuit court found that the "totality of Yost's actions, convinces us that a reasonable jury could have found Yost committed a substantial step." The court affirmed Yost's conviction.

In *United States v. Lee,* the Eleventh Circuit went further, upholding the conviction of Van Buren Lee for attempted enticement of a minor, attempted production of child pornography, and knowing receipt of child pornography. For months, Lee had communicated online with a postal inspector ("Candi Kane") posing as the "open-minded mother of two minor girls." Lee sent "Candi" and the girls sexually explicit images of himself, spoke to her by phone, and requested photographs of the girls in specific poses. Like Yost, Lee never did more than mention a willingness to travel for a proposed sexual encounter with the children. In fact, he was arrested at his own home.

On appeal, Lee argued that solely communicating with an adult intermediary did not constitute the intent necessary to support a 2422 (b) conviction, and that speech without conduct does not meet the threshold.

The circuit court disagreed. The substantial step Lee took was "toward causing assent," a mental state, not toward causing actual sexual contact. In requesting assistance from a woman who had "influence and control over the daughters," he'd crossed the line into criminality.

It was significant that one panel member, Judge Beverly B. Martin, was so unsettled by her colleagues' hair-splitting that she wrote a partial dissent, noting that Van Buren Lee had taken less of a substantial step than had any defendant in any prior case:

"I write out of concern that the majority position does not clearly demarcate despicable, but lawful talk from a criminal attempt punishable by up to thirty years in prison."

Judge Martin also acknowledged the "elephant in the room," the overwhelming fear that hung over all these cases—including Rothenberg's—the fear of predators loose on the streets.

"I did not intend to minimize the threat that sexual predators pose to children," Martin wrote. She also added that "furthering Mr. Lee's argument. . . was not an easy task."

Not an easy task. Christiansen returned to the Rothenberg appeal. Under duress (arrest, denial of bail, benzodiazepine withdrawal), Stan pleaded guilty and was never been tried before a jury of his peers. When he appealed, he didn't challenge his conviction. Instead, he contended that the district court had improperly imposed sentencing enhancements triggered by what prosecutors argued was "a pattern of prohibited sexual misconduct." The "pattern," which added eleven to twelve years to his sentence, was based on chat room conversations seized by police in Stan's apartment.

However, Christiansen noted, at no time in either conversation, did Rothenberg "indicate any desire to engage in illegal sexual conduct himself. Nor did he express any intent to meet either of the men. . . or their minor relatives. He neither initiated subsequent communications, nor indicated any intent to ensure that these sex acts occurred."

Nearly a year would pass from the date of the second conversation to Stan's encounter with Neil Spector in the FamLuv chat room, not exactly a "pattern." Stan had always insisted—and wrote to Christiansen from prison to that effect—that of the hundreds of chats seized in his condo, only a tiny fraction involve pedophilia and these were purely fantasy, his attempt to project a seductive pervy persona to the denizens of FamLuv and other forums.

Here again, the circuit court found itself facing a crucial question: Did a fantasy internet chat between Rothenberg and two adults, without further action, constitute the substantial step necessary in the commission of an "attempt" crime? If so, could this crime be further used to establish the "pattern of activity" enhancement that effectively escalated his punishment to life imprisonment?

Christiansen noted simply: "The court answered that question in the affirmative."

His analysis—supported and expanded by others familiar with the case—focused on four major problems in the Eleventh Circuit's "overbroad" interpretation:

The court mischaracterized precedent inferring a broader rule than the facts of the cited cases support. By citing *Murrell, Yost,* and *Lee* to support a conclusion that a "sexually solicitous communication by means of interstate commerce, without more, can . . . constitute a substantial step, the court ignored the evidence that these cases were factually distinguishable from Rothenberg. Yost communicated directly with someone he believed to be a minor, not an adult intermediary. His plan to meet the minor child unambiguously demonstrated his intent to engage in illegal sexual activity.

"In the two chat room conversations the prosecution used to justify sentence enhancements, Rothenberg spoke only with adult intermediaries; he never made plans to meet with his chat partners or with the minors involved and never indicated any desire to do so. He took no action—beyond participating in conversations—that would constitute an attempt 'to persuade induce, entire or coerce a minor to engage in illegal sex acts.'"

The court's interpretation of 2422 (b) runs contrary to the statute's legislative history. Tracing the statute back to its roots in the 1998 Protection of Children from Sexual Predators Act, Christiansen argued that legislators hoped *to avoid* an outcome like the one in Rothenberg. "At the very least," he insisted, "(there are) significant doubts as to whether Congress ever contemplated that the broad language of 2422 (b) could be used to incarcerate defendants who merely converse with parents or other adults about illegal sexual activity, but who take no other action." During the drafting of the Protection Act, Vermont Senator Patrick Leahy insisted criminalizing mere attempts to make contact "are prosecuting a thought crime."

The Rothenberg decision ran counter to foundational principles of criminal attempt law. Christiansen identified an alternative line of judicial reasoning running counter to the Eleventh Circuit's Murrell-Yost-Lee-Rothenberg rulings.

To make his case, Christiansen cited the Seventh Circuit's unanimous reversal of a 2422 (b) conviction— *United States v. Gladish.*

"Criminal law, because it aims at taking dangerous people out of circulation before they do harm, took a different approach (from tort law)," Chief Judge Richard Posner wrote. "A person who demonstrates by his conduct that he had the intention and capability of committing a crime was punishable, even if his plan was thwarted. The substantial step toward completion was the demonstration of dangerousness, and had been usefully described as 'some overt act adapted to, approximating, and, which in the ordinary and likely course of things, will result in the commission of the particular crime.' You were not punished just for saying that you want or even intend to kill someone, because most such talk doesn't lead to action. You have to do something that makes it reasonably clear that had you not been interrupted or made a mistake, you would have completed the crime."

"Posner's decision," Christiansen continued, "summarizes the fundamental role the *substantial step* requirement plays in balancing competing societal interests—preventative law enforcement that keeps the public safe and the individual's personal interest in avoiding punishment for unexecuted crimes . . . Rothenberg represented less than a real threat. His statements were instead more analogous to X telling Y, 'You should rob a bank.'"

Christiansen's article sent hope surging through Stan's heart. Of all the cases on all the dockets, Christiansen had chosen his! He immediately forwarded photocopies to the two judges who ruled against him. (The third, Stanley F. Birch, retired in 2010.)

None of the judges responded.

"I wouldn't doubt they simply trashed it," Stan said, "but Christiansen's work gave me renewed emphasis to fight. Finally, someone really understood what was going on, vindicating me from feeling that I was a monster of the first order, incapable of feeling."

■ ■ ■

"No one was punishable for his thoughts."

Seventy-two-year-old Stanley Rothenberg was in his ninth year of incarceration, in failing health, with scant hope for release, and was convinced that he was effectively serving life in prison for his fantasies.

DISPROPORTIONATE

As Stan shuffled into the long twilight of life in a Texas prison, the magnitude of the injustice visited upon him by a judicial system became even more apparent to him. The system he barely understood and that seemed determined to imprison him was handing down sentences far shorter to defendants whose crimes were far more virulent and harmful than Stan's misdeeds. Thanks to the same internet that had landed him in prison, he now had access to thousands of cases from courthouses all over the United States.

One of these men was Jared Fogle. Familiar to millions of Americans as the Subway Guy, Fogle was the morbidly obese young man who claimed to have lost 245 pounds on the fast-food chain's low-calorie fare. In 2015, to the absolute astonishment of his fans and sponsors, Fogle was arrested, charged, and eventually pleaded guilty to two felony sex offenses involving minor children.

For more than a decade, he'd literally been Subway's brand identity, accounting by some measures for a full 20 percent of the company's sales growth. His story, appealing boy-next-door persona, and much-publicized support of Healthy Kids clubs and other public service outreaches, so contrasted with the utter depravity of his secret, dark, and hidden life, that the Fogle case grabbed national headlines for months.

Fogle's felonies—traveling to engage in illicit sexual conduct with a minor and possession and distribution of child pornography—brought by the US Attorney for the Southern District of Indiana, were essentially identical to those that wreaked havoc on Stan except for one critical difference: Fogle's crimes, which went unnoticed for years, were far more extensive and destructive to flesh-and-blood children than any substantial step Stan had taken with an imaginary little girl.

District Judge Tanya Walton Pratt ruled that Jared Fogle, who regularly used email accounts, texts, and social networking sites to pursue underage victims, was "obsessed with sex." The same might be argued for Stan in 2008, but Fogle acted on his obsessions again and again. He cynically used his financial wherewithal and public image to prey on his victims. According to court transcripts, Fogle engaged in sexual activity with at least fourteen minor children and actively sought to have sex with victims as young as twelve. He did this for years.

Fogle produced, shared, and swapped child porn—in one instance images depicting a six-year-old—with an accomplice, Russell Taylor, who happened to run the Jared Foundation, a nonprofit founded to combat childhood obesity. At Fogle's sentencing, an outraged Judge Pratt declared "the level of perversion and lawlessness exhibited by Mr. Fogle was extreme."

Fogle faced up to fifty years in prison. And yet, as part of a plea bargain arrangement, federal prosecutors recommend a twelve-year prison sentence (compared with enhancements that put sixty-four-year-old Rothenberg away for twenty-five years). Judge Pratt literally overrode prosecution recommendations for a less severe sentence, sending the thirty-eight-year-old Fogle to prison for fifteen years and eight months. With good behavior, he could be paroled after thirteen years.

According to press reports, Fogle left the Birch Bayh Federal Building in Indianapolis, "blowing kisses to family members."

Of course, the other significant difference between

Fogle's case and Stan's was that Fogle had a plea bargain in place before he pleaded guilty. Stan did not.

■ ■ ■

The issue of Stanley Rothenberg's over-sentencing was again raised in the prosecution and conviction of Donald H. Gates. Again, Rothenberg's nemesis, Port St. Lucie Detective Neil Spector, played a part. Working under-cover for the Internet Crimes Against Children (ICAC) South Florida Task Force, Spector assumed the persona of "Joey," a fifteen-year-old boy. According to court documents, an adult male (later identified as Donald Gates) approached "Joey" in a chat room set up to facilitate sex between minors and older men. The two exchanged a series of blunt messages in the sexual shorthand favored by chat room denizens.

According to testimony later presented in federal court, Gates initiated the chat room contact with Spector. He blew past a warning flag when "Joey" revealed he was underage and pressed "Joey" about past sexual encounters with older men. In a follow-up phone conversation (Spector enlisted a college-age volunteer for the "Joey" role), Gates detailed his homosexual trysts with "A. K.," a sixteen-year-old Connecticut boy. He ended the exchange after arranging to meet "Joey" for dinner, a movie, and oral sex.

Gates was arrested at the scene of the proposed encounter. He was charged with violating 18 USC. § 2422 (b), an attempt to "persuade, induce, entice, or coerce a minor to engage in sexual activity," the same felony Rothenberg faced. It was noteworthy that Gates went beyond anything Rothenberg attempted. He literally showed up to meet "Joey" with a porno movie.

At Gates' two-day trial, prosecutors had little trouble convincing a jury that Gates had taken the substantial step required by the felony statute. His boasting about prior sexual encounters with the underage "A. K." became evidence of a pattern of criminal behavior. Upon conviction, Gates appealed. One of his grounds for appeal alleged that Neil Spector entrapped him.

In the fall of 2009, his conviction was affirmed by the Eleventh Circuit. His sentence was eleven years in prison, less than half of Stan's.

■ ■ ■

The evidence of injustice in Stan's sentence continued to pile up. In 2003, a violent sex offender named Edgar Joe Searcy pleaded guilty in district court (Southern District of Florida) to using interstate commerce to engage in sexual activity with a minor—another violation of 18 USC. §2422 (b). Searcy had a prior conviction in Kansas for "sexually exploiting a child" and another in Florida for "committing a lewd, lascivious, or indecent act upon a child." Taken together, these convictions make him as a career criminal "unable to refrain from engaging in sex offenses with minors."

In Miami, the district court judge tacked on the justifiable "pattern of criminal behavior" enhancement to his sentence. Searcy appealed. In December 2003, the Eleventh Circuit Court affirmed Searcy's conviction. His sentence: fifteen years in prison.

■ ■ ■

In 2015, a Texas resident named LaDestro "Derek" Douglas pleaded guilty to "conspiracy to commit sex trafficking of children," an understatement of Douglas's evildoing. He was the internet predator every parent dreads. According to court documents and press reports, in the spring of 2012, Douglas, a small-time pimp, started an IM conversation with a fragile seventeen-year-old girl living in a foster home. He persuaded the girl to leave Alabama and travel to join him in Dallas. Douglas next photographed the girl, posted lascivious pictures of her on sex websites, accepted solicitations for her services, and drove her to Odessa and other Texas cities to engage in sex acts.

At the time of his arrest, Douglas had procured two other minor girls, both runaways, to his sex trafficking operation. At his sentencing, US District Judge Barbara M. G. Lynn declared the case was not about prostitution, but the sale and degradation of children. "To call it human trafficking acknowledges the horror of what you were doing," Lynn said.

For his crimes, Douglas was sentenced to fifteen years in prison—60 percent of Stanley Rothenberg's sentence.

■ ■ ■

The cases were endless. They offered a look into the dark side of Western culture and media where children have been exploited as sex objects for decades. Calvin Klein's underwear ads were the most familiar, but more recently an ad appeared in a national magazine portraying a girl, no more than eleven, wearing a fur, high heels, and makeup. The headline: "Get what you've always wanted."

It is the same society that calls child molesters into being and then excoriates their existence.

LUFKIN, TEXAS BOYS & GIRLS CLUB

Acting on a tip, police discovered numerous images of child porn on the office computer of Patrick Sanders, director of the Lufkin, Texas Boys & Girls Club. It turned out that Sanders, fifty-two, had persuaded a seventeen-year-old male to pose nude for him and later loaded the images onto his computer. Sanders worked for the national youth organization for thirteen years. The news of his arrest sent waves of fear and outrage rippling across East Texas. In an interview prior his arrest, Sanders had even bragged about his role at the club. "The children," he said, "This is where it all begins. We have a chance to shape and mold them, and they'll never forget you."

He was charged with three counts of possession of child pornography and three counts of "sexual performance by a child," all felonies. He pleaded guilty and was sentenced to four years and four months in federal prison.

THE CACHE

Michael "DublHelix" Baratta, William Watkins, Marc "Kingbee" Reeder, and Scott Van Dorp operated the *Cache*, the largest child porn-swapping website ever created, for ten years until a lengthy investigation by Interpol, the FBI, and local law enforcement finally shut down the online bulletin board.

In its heyday, 1,500 *Cache* members anonymously produced and shared millions of child porn images and videos. Reeder described the *Cache* as "a place where we traded links to images of underage girls, nude underage girls." According to the Justice Department, a number of *Cache* members posted images of children they'd raped and molested. For security, the site was encrypted and password protected. (Indeed, law enforcement investigators discovered *Cache* forums advising members how to avoid detection.) Meanwhile, the sordid circumstances and fate of the thousands of vulnerable children in scores of countries raised no concern to bulletin board users

Ultimately, all four men pleaded guilty in district court in Indianapolis. Reeder, who testified that he personally possessed hundreds of thousands (200 gigabytes) of child porn images, was sentenced to ten years in prison. Baratta and Watkins, top level *Cache* administrators, drew fifteen years, as did Scott Van Dorp who ran a second child porn board, inappropriately named *Country Lounge,* in Nashville. Van Dorp's child porn stash reportedly contained one million images.

Delwyn Savigar, the British mastermind of the *Cache*, was sentenced to fourteen years in prison (slightly more than half of Stanley Rothenberg's sentence) for creating what was essentially a massive engine of child abuse and human exploitation. In the UK, Savigar also stands convicted of raping two thirteen-year-old girls.

A COUNTER TREND

In 2014, during a sting operation, FBI agents remotely accessed Raul Vazquez's home computer. They uncovered images and videos of adult males engaged in sex with children, including two girls, ages three and five. A search of Vasquez's Brooklyn home turned up additional child porn images on a thumb drive, as well as evidence that Vasquez, a fifty-three-year-old restaurant manager and father of five, had engaged in sexting with children.

There was no evidence that Vasquez had made or sold child pornography or attempted to contact minors. He eventually pleaded guilty of violating the same statute used to indict Stanley Rothenberg.

"I prayed to God and took my chances," Vasquez told *NBC News.*

Under the Sentencing Guidelines, Vasquez faced ten years in prison. His Presentence Report recommended six-and-a-half to eight years. In a decision that undoubtedly sent shockwaves through the Justice Department, District Judge Jack Weinstein sentenced Vazquez to five days (time already served), plus seven years of supervision.

The ruling stunned legal observers and triggered a flurry of outraged tabloid headlines ("Judge Gives Man 5 Days for Child Porn, Rails Against Harsh Sentences," "Man Convicted of Child Porn in Brooklyn Set Free After Five Days in Jail"). In truth, it was Judge Weinstein who was outraged. Like a growing number of district court judges, he'd long been an opponent of the Guidelines that limited a judge's ability to take into account compounding or mitigating circumstances and impose sentences accordingly. Vasquez provided Weinstein an opportunity to distinguish between offenders who pose a clear and present danger to children and those who simply do not. It was a distinction well worth noting.

"The existing guidelines do not adequately balance the need to protect the public and juveniles in particular,"

Weinstein wrote, "against the need to avoid excessive punishment.

In his ninety-eight-page decision, Weinstein argued
that "Removing Raul Vasquez from his family will not
further the interests of justice. It will cause serious harm
to his children by depriving them of a loving father and
role model and will strip Raul Vasquez of the opportunity
to heal through continued, sustained treatment and the
support of close family."

Weinstein's was a rare articulation of the argument that
nonviolent sex offenders were often mentally ill and in need
of treatment rather than despised criminals to be punished
and banished from society. Clearly there are monsters—
like Cache founder Delwyn Savigar—who exploit children
and should be taken off the streets, but the push and pull
between harsh punishment and a nuanced approach to
psychologically impaired, nonthreatening individuals like
Vazquez and Stanley Rothenburg continues.

But compare the actual details of the crimes committed here with the sexually titillating but non-contact
details of *United States v. Stanley G. Rothenberg* and ask
yourself this question: what is justice?

THE POST-BOOKER SENTENCING LANDSCAPE

On a tip from US Postal Service inspectors, federal agents
used a battering ram to smash into the Capitol Hill townhouse of thirty-three-year-old Jesse Ryan Loskarn. After
child porn was discovered on his computer, Loskarn was
charged with possession and distribution of child pornography. His arrest generated lurid headlines and sent
waves of gossip and speculation reverberating through

the Capitol. The flesh-and-blood Ryan Loskarn, whoever he was, disappeared.

At first glance, the raid heralded another victory in the Justice Department's grinding war against online child abusers. Another dangerous pedophile would be tried, convicted, sentenced, and taken off the streets. Vulnerable children would be safe. Parents could sleep easier.

And then something changed. The news stories ("The Predator Next Door" variety) proved to be exaggerations. Loskarn was the chief of staff for Tennessee's US Senator Lamar Alexander. Rather than a monster reflected in the sickly glow of a computer monitor, he was well-regarded, outgoing, a savvy political operative with a promising future. (The same process of dehumanization transformed Stanley Rothenberg who to this day pleads, "I'm not the monster society had deemed me.") As far as the evidence indicated, Loskarn himself had never touched a flesh-and-blood child—but he'd been a victim of abuse himself.

In January 2014, as prosecutors were putting together their case, Loskarn refused to be part of the spectacle. He was found dead in the basement of his parents' Maryland home, an apparent suicide by hanging. He left a note attempting to explain how his self-loathing and shame metastasized into something darker. For the first time, the public learned that Loskarn himself had been a victim of abuse.

"I found myself drawn to the videos that matched my childhood abuse," he wrote. "It was painful and humiliating to admit to myself, let alone the whole world, but I pictured myself as a child in the image or video. The more an image mirrors some element of my memories and took me back, the more I felt a connection. This was my deepest, darkest secret."

■ ■ ■

The connections between prior abuse and becoming an abuser were increasingly being recognized by courts, but it was too late for Ryan Loskarn and maybe for Stanley Rothenberg. There's evidence to suggest that a handful of federal judges, supported by new research into nonviolent sex offenders and pedophiles, have begun to bypass the draconian punishments of the Guidelines. They've begun to back away from the cruel and unusual punishments handed down to thousands of individuals over the last decades.

The DOJ remains relentless in hunting down internet predators. In 2009, it brought 2,300 prosecutions for possessing (downloading) and distributing (sharing) child porn, the highest number ever recorded. Yet, that same year, only 44 percent of all federal child porn convictions resulted in sentences within the Guidelines' recommendation. By 2012, the figure had dropped to 33 percent.

In 2004, by contrast, the US Sentencing Commission (which formulates the Guidelines) reported that nearly 80 percent of sentences for such individuals came in at, or even above, the Guidelines' recommendations.

In part, these judges were responding to a landmark 2005 Supreme Court ruling (*United States v. Booker*) that makes the Guidelines advisory rather than mandatory. (Implemented as part of the 1984 Comprehensive Crime Control Act, the Guidelines were an attempt to "provide certainty and fairness. . .by avoiding unwanted disparity among offenders of similar characteristics convicted of similar criminal conduct, while permitting sufficient judicial flexibility to take into account relevant aggravating and mitigating factors."

It was increasingly clear that they have not suc-ceeded. Worse, the pursuit of certainty often brings unintended consequences. This had been most obvious in the so-called War on Drugs. In the thirty years since the passage of the Anti-Drug Abuse Act, which ensured mandatory minimum sentences for drug violations, the United States penal population had grown from about 300,000 to more than two million; more than half were incarcerated for drug offenses. Disproportionately, these were minorities and the poor.

For some judges, there was no question that the Guide-lines helped simplify the task (responsibility) of distilling justice from the endless complexity of human misbehav-ior into a one-size-fits-all paradigm. Other jurists, and they are legion, viewed the Guidelines as impeding their sworn obligation to act as unbiased and fair arbiters, dis-pensing justice to each individual standing before the bar.

The late Anthony Alaimo, chief judge for the Southern District of Georgia, a man renowned for his integrity and fairness, struggled for years over the sentences the Guide-lines forced him to impose. One trial in particular stood out in Alaimo's memory more than a decade after its conclusion. In 1998, a federal grand jury indicted four top executives of LCP Chemicals on forty-two counts of conspiring to violate the Clean Water Act and a half-dozen other environmental protection statutes. For more than fifty years, LCP dumped toxic chemicals into the marshes and estuaries north of the city of Brunswick. More than 800 acres were poisoned to the point that the EPA eventually declared it a Super-fund site. To this day, the LCP case was regarded as one of the worst instances of corporate negligence in history. Hence, the Justice Department pursued a criminal indict-ment against the CEO and his managers.

As Alaimo remembered it, among those indicted were Christian Hansen, former chairman of LCP's holding company, and his son, Randall Hansen, the company's executive vice president. After a two-week trial and despite the efforts of a battery of top defense attorneys Christian Hansen was convicted on forty-one counts of conspiracy and additional violations. The jury found Randall guilty on thirty-four counts. In the course of the trial, Alaimo said, the evidence indicated that "the father, who'd been the CEO, had induced his son, a Harvard Business School graduate, to come Georgia to try to salvage the business. The cost of it was they both got convicted."

Despite considerable mitigating evidence, the guidelines prevented Alaimo from handing down (as he felt the evidence warranted) a nuanced sentence for Randall Hansen. After trying (and delaying for weeks) to justify a "downward departure," the judge finally realized his hands were tied. "I simply could not make such a finding," Alaimo said.

The dilemma was particularly wrenching for Alaimo, who'd spent years as a POW in a Nazi stalag during World War II and fully understood the corrosive effects of incarceration. Decades later, the case still troubled him.

"It was really heartrending," Alaimo said. "The son had an impeccable background. He was the ideal kind of parent, always with his kids. His wife made one of the most impassioned speeches I'd ever heard. I knew nothing could be accomplished by incarcerating this man, but nonetheless, it was the law. I sent him away for four years."

■ ■ ■

Freed of the Guidelines, district judges like Jack Weinstein were no longer forced to impose fifteen- to twenty-five-year sentences on internet offenders who have never been contact child molesters. (No jurists believe such defendants should go unpunished.) In Chicago, for example, federal prosecutors sought a twenty- to twenty-four-year sentence for a man convicted of downloading child pornography. District Judge Joan Gottschall of the Northern District of Illinois sentenced him to six years plus long-term court supervision.

"These guidelines were flawed," Gottschall told the *Wall Street Journal*, "not only because they were duplicative and draconian, but most critically, because they apply to almost all offenders, allowing no distinction between aggravated and less aggravated behavior."

To some observers, this inability to temper justice with mercy reflects the paranoid style rampant in 2016 America characterized by overwhelming fear, rage, distrust, suspicion, and vengefulness. As written, the laws used to convict and incarcerate individuals like Stanley Rothenberg make no distinction between real monsters, in this case, hardcore contact predators prowling for children and damaged individuals like Rothenberg, who were certifiably mentally ill and would benefit from therapy as well as punishment.

"The legislative scheme underlying current child pornography laws in the US goes much further than addressing the actual harm caused by viewing or possessing such images," argues Andrew Extein, executive director of The Center For Sexual Justice, an advocacy group. "These sentences address imaginary assertions that those who view or download such illicit images were also guilty of undiscovered abuse in the past or will commit heinous contact offenses in the future."

Extein's argument was reflected in the egregious 2011 prosecution of a stockroom clerk named Daniel Guevara Vilca, who was arrested for possession of child pornography. Like Rothenberg, Vilca refused a plea bargain offer. As a result, Florida prosecutors treated each of the 454 images discovered on Vilca's computer's hard drive as a separate felony (a throwback to the pre-digital era where such a stash would have represented an extensive pattern of criminal behavior). After he was convicted in a jury trial, Collier Circuit Judge Fred Hardt sentenced twenty-six-year-old Vilca (who had no prior criminal history) to 150 years in prison, a punishment typically reserved for heinous first-degree murderers.

John Grisham, author of dozens of best-selling legal thrillers, spoke out against this kind of over-sentencing in a 2014 interview with the British newspaper *The Telegraph*. "We have prisons now filled with guys my age," Grisham said. "Sixty-year-old white men who've never harmed anybody, would never touch a child. But they got online one night and started surfing around, probably had too much to drink or whatever, and pushed the wrong buttons, went too far, and got into child porn."

"There's so many, that they put them in the same prison like they were a bunch of perverts. We've gone nuts with this incarceration...I have no sympathy for real pedophiles. God, please lock those people up! But many of these guys do not deserve harsh prison sentences, and that's what they were getting."

In response, Grisham was viciously attacked on social media and elsewhere for daring to give voice to thousands of men like Stanley Rothenberg and Daniel Vilca; he had to pull back his statement.

CIRCUIT COURTS

In 2011, the circuit courts, bombarded by thousands of direct appeals in such cases began to weigh in. That year, Ninth Circuit Judge Stephen Reinhardt was compelled to speak out not only on over-sentencing, but also to attempt to address the deep-seated issues he believes many of these offenders struggle with:

"I do not profess to know the solution of how to cure the illness that causes otherwise law-abiding people to engage in the viewing of child pornography," Reinhardt said. "Psychological impairment is, in most if not all cases, the cause of the criminal conduct. Those who only view child pornography, including those who exchange computer video files, were in all likelihood the victims of a form of mental illness that prevents them from controlling what they would otherwise understand not only to be unhealthy impulses, but impulses that result in great harm to the most innocent members of our society.

"I know only that a lengthy sentence—ten years for a first offense—cannot be the answer. Such a sentence serves only to create another class of people with ruined lives—victims of serious mental illness whom society should instead attempt to treat in a constructive and humane manner."

As it turned out, Daniel Vilca's case did raise an outcry among sentence reform proponents and legal observers, among them, Douglas Berman, an Ohio State University law professor, who reviewed the case on his respected *Sentencing and Law Policy* blog: "To me, a failure to distinguish between people who look at these dirty pictures and people who commit contact offenses, lacks the proportionality I think our law demands."

Vilca was granted some relief. In the summer of 2014, the Florida Second District Court of Appeals reversed his conviction and ordered a retrial.

■ ■ ■

The winds of change have been slow to reach the federal penal system. Sex offenders in general were the bottom of the prisoner hierarchy, pedophiles the lowest of the low. Stan, a gay man convicted of a sex crime involving children, was lower still.

In FCI Seagoville, a guard discovered that inmate Daniel Borgos (a New Yorker convicted of distributing child porn) had in his possession a copy of *Kidskin COMIXX*. According to newspaper reports of the incident, *Kidskin* was a crude, thirty-seven-page handmade comic book depicting an adult male "engaging in sexually explicit conduct with three girls between the ages of six and eleven."

When questioned, Borgos said the comic was created and circulated by another inmate. At the time, he was scheduled to be released in two years; instead, he was re-indicted for being in "receipt of obscene visual representations of the sexual abuse of children."

To bring a possession of child pornography charge, the "child" must exist somewhere; however, drawings, paintings, writings, sculptures, and other sexual depictions of children lacking scientific, literary, artistic, or political value fall under a 2003 federal obscenity law known as the Protect

Act. In 2008, a federal appeals court upheld the nation's first conviction under that law.

Burgos was twenty-seven years old. *Kidskin COMIXX* was offensive, crude, repugnant, and obscene. In some circles, it might be considered a gross-out series of sketches drawn by high school slacker. Nonetheless, in October 2015, US District Judge David C. Godbey tacked an additional ten years to Borgos' sentence.

To deprive a man already paying a hard debt to society ten years of his life seems equally obscene. "These laws were intended to protect actual people," insists James Cantor, a professor of psychiatry and a pedophilia expert at the University of Toronto. "When we're talking about a drawing, who was the victim? We feel these things were icky, but icky was not a real reason to pass a law."

THE SENTENCING COMMISSION

At the moment, nearly 750,000 Americans are listed as sex offenders. Men like Rothenberg have discovered that paying their debt to society can extend beyond temporal limits. If purgatory represents a time-limited state of penitence, they are in hell—imprisoned, subject to eternal abuse by inmates and staff, and thrown in the hole (solitary confinement) for their protection. Physically safe but emotionally and psychologically devastated as the foundations of their lives—careers, relationships, and families—crumble into dust.

Free of prison, there is little relief: After parole and probation, they are listed in sex offender registries, typically for the rest of their lives. (In 1994, the Jacob Wetterling Crimes Against Children and Sexually Violent Offender

Registration Act required all states to establish stringent registration programs for sex offenders. Megan's Law [1996] mandates states develop notification protocols allowing public access to information about sex offenders in the community.) These listings, which include mugshots, home addresses, and descriptions of the crime, make it nearly impossible to find work or housing. Once publicly identified, they and their families are subject to continuous threats and harassment. In many communities, sex offenders are forbidden from living within 1,000 yards of schools and public parks.

In the face of such discrimination, a handful of them make their way to literal communities comprised of other sex offenders. Miracle Village, a ramshackle "safe haven" in the Florida Everglades, shelters more than 200 such individuals and their families.

WHERE WAS IT ALL GOING?

"I'm not suggesting that someone who looks at child pornography should just walk," Troy Stabenow, a Missouri public defender who had researched the human cost of massive over-sentencing, told *The New York Times*. "But we ought to punish people for what they do, not for our fear…We've reached a critical moment for change. The recent sentences were signaling as strongly as I have ever seen that judges around the country think the current system was broken."

In 2013, Judge Patti B. Sarris, chief of the United States Sentencing Commission, acknowledged as much in a *Time* magazine interview. "Because of the changes in the use of internet-based technologies," Sarris said, "the existing penalty structure was in need of revision."

DISPARITIES IN SEX OFFENSE SENTENCING

In Ascending Order of Severity of Sentencing

	CRIMINAL CODE VIOLATION	SENTENCE	NO. OF VICTIMS
STANLEY ROTHENBERG, 64			
Former CEO of Furniture Co. Federal Case (2008) Southern District of Florida	18 USC 2422(b) and 18 USC 2252 (a) (4)(b) Solicitation of a minor for sex and possession of 97 images of child porn. No Plea Agreement. Open Plea.	25 Years $25,000 Fine Lifetime supervision upon release. Plus lifetime registration.	None

ROBERT RICHARDS, IV, 48			
Grandson of iconic DuPont family State of Delaware Case (2009)	Second-degree rape of 3-year old daughter, (mandatory minimum of ten years in prison). Defendant pleaded down to 1 count of 4th degree rape which carries NO specific term.	Suspended*	1
*Judge Jan R. Jurden suspended 8-year prison term to probation citing defendant would not 'fare well' in prison.			

	CRIMINAL CODE VIOLATION	SENTENCE	NO. OF VICTIMS
JEFFREY EPSTEIN			
Billionaire money tycoon State of Florida case (2007)	Original federal charge of 'sex trafficking' which would net 20 year sentence. Dropped by Feds so that Epstein could plead down to a state of Florida charge of "Procuring a person under the age of 18 for prostitution."	1 year, 6 months	≈ 24
DENNIS HASTERT			
Third In Line to the Presidency of the United States. Federal Case	Unlawful structuring of bank withdrawals and making false statements to the FBI. Allegations of sexual misconduct that detailed specific and graphic incidents on at least 4 boys in the 1970s. Statute of Limitations prevented prosecution.	1 year, 3 months	4
ANTHONY WEINER			
Former member of US House of Representatives Federal Case (2016/2017)	Accused of transmitting explicit photos of himself to several underage girls as young as 15. Pleaded guilty to a single charge of transferring obscene material to a minor though a plea agreement.	1 year, 9 months	> 1
ANTHONY MURRELL			
Federal Case (2002) Southern District of Florida	18 USC 2422(b) - Use of Interstate Commerce to solicit minor for sex. Nabbed in a sting by same undercover officer as Rothenberg and sentenced by the same Judge Graham.	2 years, 9 months	None
DONALD GATES			
Federal Case (2009) Southern District of Florida*	Same as Murrell above	11 years, 3 months	None

* Same as Rothenberg

	CRIMINAL CODE VIOLATION	SENTENCE	NO. OF VICTIMS
ROBERT C LATHAM, 51			
CEO of Timber Company Federal Case (2003) Southern District of Florida	Same as Murrell above	11 years, 3 months	None
EDGAR JOE SCEARCY			
Federal Case (2003) Southern District of Florida*	18 USC 2422 (b) Use of interstate commerce to solicit a minor for sex. Similar sting to Rothenberg; different sentencing judge.	15 years*	> 3
* Received upward departure due to being categorized as a career criminal.			
JARED FOGLE			
Former pitchman for Subway Federal Case 2015-2016 (Net worth > $15 million)	Paying for sex with minor girls. Receipt and distribution of child pornography.	15 years, 8 months	14
LARRY NASSAR, 53			
Osteopathic physician For US Gymnastic Team Federal case (2017)	Pleaded guilty to 3 counts—all related to child pornography including possession. 37,000 images + videos recovered. Other charges pending.	Plea Agreement for 22–27 years	125
JERRY SANDUSKY			
Former Penn State Football Coach Commonwealth of PA case.	8 Counts of involuntary sexual intercourse; 7 Counts of indecent assault; 9 Counts of unlawful contact with minors; 10 Counts of endangering the welfare of children.	30 to 60 years	7

85731271R00166